In case of loss, please return to:

_____

_____

_____

_____

As a reward: $ _____

D1280432

CHASE the LION

{stepping confidently into the unknown}

by MARK BATTERSON

Published by LifeWay Press®
© 2007 Mark Batterson

ISBN: 978-1-4158-6101-1
Item Number: 005100606

Dewey Decimal Classification Number: 152.4
Subject Heading: FEAR \ COURAGE \ CHRISTIAN LIFE

Printed in the United States of America.

Leadership and Adult Publishing
LifeWay Church Resources
One LifeWay Plaza
Nashville, Tennessee 37234-0175

We believe the Bible has God for its author; salvation for its end; and truth, without any mixture of error, for its matter and that all Scripture is totally true and trustworthy. The 2000 statement of The Baptist Faith and Message is our doctrinal guideline.

TABLE of CONTENTS

Introduction   Defying Odds 8
Impossible odds set the stage for amazing miracles.

Session 1   Taking Risks 12
Small acts of courage change the course of history.

Session 2   Seizing Opportunities 28
Prayer has a way of turning problems into opportunities.

Session 3   Facing Fears 44
Jesus wants to recondition our fear with faith.

Session 4   Reframing Problems 62
Who you become is not determined by your circumstances.

Session 5   Embracing Uncertainties 78
Uncertainty is the point where faith enters the equation.

Session 6   Looking Foolish 96
Growing in Christ changes self-consciousness to God-consciousness.

MEET THE AUTHOR
MARK BATTERSON

Thanks for picking up your copy of *Chase the Lion*. My name is Mark Batterson, and I live on Capitol Hill with my wife Lora and three kids: Parker, Summer, and Josiah. Before moving to D.C., I grew up in the Chicago area and went to school at the University of Chicago, Central Bible College, and then Trinity Evangelical Divinity School.

For the past decade I've had the privilege of serving as lead pastor of National Community Church (*www.theaterchurch.com*) in Washington, D.C. Focused on reaching emerging generations, 73 percent of NCCers are single 20-somethings and 70 percent come from an unchurched or dechurched background. We are currently one church with four locations and the vision of NCC is to meet in movie theaters at metro stops throughout the metro D.C. area.

If you enjoy *Chase the Lion*, I'd love to continue the conversation via my blog at *www.evotional.com*, or my book, *In a Pit with a Lion on a Snowy Day*.

SPECIAL THANKS FROM MARK

I want to thank the entire Threads team for making *Chase the Lion* a reality. I also want to say a special thanks to Heather Zempel. Heather oversees leadership development and discipleship at National Community Church. I don't know anyone more passionate about the discipleship potential of small groups! Without her help, this study never would have seen the light of day.

DEFYING ODDS

★★★★★★★

"BENAIAH SON OF JEHOIADA WAS THE SON OF A BRAVE MAN FROM KABZEEL,
a man of many exploits. Benaiah killed two sons of Ariel of Moab, and he went down into a pit on a snowy day and killed a lion. He also killed an Egyptian, a huge man. Even though the Egyptian had a spear in his hand, Benaiah went down to him with a club, snatched the spear out of the Egyptian's hand, and then killed him with his own spear. These were the exploits of Benaiah son of Jehoiada, who had a reputation among the three warriors. He was the most honored of the Thirty, but he did not become one of the Three. David put him in charge of his bodyguard" (2 Samuel 23:20-23).

Let me state the obvious: Benaiah was not the odds-on favorite in any of these encounters. He was doubled-teamed by two mighty Moabites—a two-to-one underdog. If I'm placing bets on an average size Israelite with a club or a giant Egyptian with a spear, I'm going to put my money on the sharp, pointy thing. I can't even imagine how you begin to calculate the odds of man vs. lion.

Not only do fully grown lions weigh up to 500 pounds and run 35 mph, but their eyesight is five times better than a human with 20/20 vision. This lion had a huge advantage in a dimly lit pit, and I guarantee that a sure-footed lion with feline reflexes certainly gains the upper paw in snowy, slippery conditions.

Most of us don't like being in pits with lions on snowy days, but those are the stories worth telling. Those are the experiences that make life worth living.

Lion-chasers don't try to avoid situations where the odds are against them. Lion-chasers know that impossible odds set the stage for amazing miracles.

Here's the rest of the story: finding yourself in a pit with a lion on a snowy day seems to qualify as bad luck or a bad day. But stop and think about it—can't you just see David flipping through résumés looking for a bodyguard? *I majored in security at Jerusalem U.* Nope. *I did an internship with the temple guard.* Don't call us; we'll call you. *I worked for Brinks Armored Chariots.* Thanks, but no thanks. Then he comes to Benaiah's résumé: *I killed a lion in a pit on a snowy day.* You've got to admit that looks awfully good on your résumé if you're applying for a bodyguard position with the king of Israel.

What seemed like a bad break turned into a big opportunity, and those impossible odds set the stage for his entire military career.

I think part of us wants God to reduce the obstacles. We like situations where the odds are in our favor. But sometimes God allows the odds to be stacked against us so He can reveal more of His glory through it.

MAYBE BENAIAH KNEW HE WASN'T OUTNUMBERED BY THE MOABITES. HE HAD THE FATHER, SON, AND HOLY SPIRIT ON HIS SIDE! A GIANT EGYPTIAN CAN'T STAND UP TO THE GOD OF ISRAEL. AND A BIG CAT IS NO MATCH FOR THE LION OF THE TRIBE OF JUDAH.

Benaiah's boldness was not just a function of his courage; it was a function of his confidence in God. His God was bigger than armies, weapons, and even nature. Because his God was that big, none of the situations were problems—they were just opportunities for a big God to showcase His big power.

So how big is your God?

Is He bigger than your biggest problem? Is He bigger than your worst failure? Is He bigger than your greatest fear?

We could easily look at someone like Benaiah and call him reckless. We might very sensibly argue that he acted without thinking, or that his actions were not very prudent in that specific situation. But what if our arguments against risk-takers like Benaiah are rooted deeply in the smallness of our own God?

The world is full of cautious and prudent people who will live fine, long lives. But chances are if you spend your life in an attempt to eliminate risk, uncertainty, and fear you will miss out on some of the most amazing experiences a person can have with Jesus.

Your greatest regret at the end of your life will be the lions you didn't chase. You will look back longingly on the risks not taken, opportunities not seized, and dreams not pursued. Stop running away from what scares you, and start chasing the God-ordained opportunities that cross your path.

Over the next six sessions, we are going to explore some lion-chasing skills. We'll be challenged to take risks and seize opportunities. We will face fears and reframe the problems in our lives. We will embrace uncertainty and look foolish in order to defy the odds and pursue the God-given callings and passions of our lives.

IN WHAT AREAS OF LIFE ARE YOU CURRENTLY FACING IMPOSSIBLE ODDS?

WHAT LION DO YOU NEED TO CHASE OVER THE NEXT SEVERAL WEEKS?

Let's be clear, though. The goal here is not for you to take a risk simply for the sake of taking a risk. It's not for you to have a life of adventure just because that's the only kind of life worth living. The goal here is all of us to begin to live intentionally, not once but in every moment of our lives.

THE END RESULT IS NOT FOR YOU TO CHASE A SINGLE LION; THE END RESULT IS FOR YOU TO BECOME A LION-CHASER.

Get ready to stop casually walking through life hoping for an opportunity to take hold of you. It's time to live intentionally. It's time to live purposefully. It's time to stop letting circumstances bully you around. It's time to chase the lion!

LET'S GET STARTED.

take *{verb}*: to accept and act upon or comply with

risk *{noun}*: a hazard or dangerous chance

ON OCTOBER 31, 1517, a monk named Martin Luther approached the Castle Church in Wittenberg, Germany, and nailed a piece of paper to the church doors. His 95 theses attacked the practice of indulgences—the selling of forgiveness by the church. Luther was put on trial, and he was excommunicated from the church. But that one act of courage had a domino effect—it ignited the Protestant Reformation.

On April 18, 1945, a factory owner named Oskar Schindler began to circulate a manually typed list of 1,097 names—297 women and 800 men who he would rescue from Nazi concentration camps. Schindler lost everything, and he died broke. But that one act of courage had a domino effect—a half-century later, there are more than 6,000 descendants of the Schindlerjuden.

On December 1, 1951, a seamstress named Rosa Parks stepped on a bus in Montgomery, Alabama. Segregation laws required black passengers to give up their seats for white passengers. Rosa Parks refused to do so. She was arrested. She lost her job. But that one act of courage had a domino effect—it inspired a citywide boycott and a court battle. Within two years, bus segregation was ruled unconstitutional.

I'm neither a historian nor the son of a historian, but let me make an observation: small acts of courage change the course of history. Someone is willing to take a risk, and that risk has a domino effect.

TAKING RISKS

SESSION ONE

THE DOMINO EFFECT

We think about people like Martin Luther, Oskar Schindler, and Rosa Parks in heroic terms, but they didn't know they were making history when they were making history! They were just ordinary people taking risks. When you take a chance, you never know what ripples will come from it.

List some ordinary people from your life who have taken risky actions. What did they do? What was the risk? What were the results?

Download the *Chase the Lion* playlist to use as your soundtrack for this study. Get the list from your group leader or at *www.threadsmedia.com/media.*

What risks have you taken in your own life? What were the results?

What is the difference between good risk and bad risk?

There is a strange little story of a great risk taker recorded in 2 Samuel 23. An ancient warrior named Benaiah chased a lion into a pit on a snowy day and killed it:

"Benaiah son of Jehoiada was the son of a brave man from Kabzeel, a man of many exploits. Benaiah killed two sons of Ariel of Moab, and he went down into a pit on a snowy day and killed a lion. He also killed an Egyptian, a huge man. Even though the Egyptian had a spear in his hand, Benaiah went down to him with a club, snatched the spear out of the Egyptian's hand, and then killed him with his own spear. These were the exploits of Benaiah son of Jehoiada, who had a reputation among the three warriors" (2 Samuel 23:20-22).

Scripture goes on to list Benaiah's military achievements, and they are pretty impressive. He was one of the most decorated and celebrated warriors in Israel's history. He was the captain of King David's bodyguard. He was one of David's 30 mighty men. In fact, Scripture says he was more honored than the other 30. Benaiah went on to become commander-in-chief of Israel's army.

The genealogy of success can always be traced back to the risks we take. 2 Samuel 23 records three risk "dominos." Benaiah took on two Moabites despite being outnumbered; he chased a lion despite snowy conditions; and he fought an Egyptian despite being out-armed. Those three risks had a domino effect on his life as well as the lives of those around him.

As I reflect on my own life, I realize that most of the good things that have happened are the by-product of a few risks. Even further, it seems to me that the bigger the risks the bigger the eventual rewards.

RISKY BUSINESS

The Bible is the story of risk takers—ordinary people who took extraordinary risks. Take Daniel as another example. Daniel was part of the best and brightest Israelites who were exiled to a foreign nation.

Recognizing Daniel's aptitude, Darius the Mede elevated him to a position of high authority. Unfortunately, the other administrators were jealous of Daniel's power. After looking for something that they could use to discredit him, they finally decided the only thing they could accuse him of was faithfulness to his religion.

They orchestrated a law outlawing the worship of anyone or anything except Darius. Anyone who disobeyed this law would be executed. Daniel had to make a choice; would he play it safe, or would he take a risk?

"When Daniel learned that the document had been signed, he went into his house. The windows in its upper room opened toward Jerusalem, and three times a day he got down on his knees, prayed, and gave thanks to his God, just as he had done before. Then these men went as a group and found Daniel petitioning and imploring his God" (Daniel 6:10-11).

What did Daniel get for his risk? In the short run, he got a one-way ticket to the lions' den. But when God entered the equation and shut the mouths of the lions, Darius himself honored Daniel's God and decreed that his entire kingdom should do the same. The world was changed because Daniel took a risk.

Daniel, whose name means "God is my judge," was born around 623 B.C. during the reign of King Josiah. In 586 B.C., the Babylonians invaded Judah, captured Jerusalem, and began to deport the Jewish people throughout the Babylonian Empire. As a teenager, Daniel was deported during the first of three major exiles.

Peter, originally named "Simon" (meaning "hearer") became famous for his big mouth and zealous faith. He grew up on the Sea of Galilee and worked as a fisherman until he answered Jesus' call to follow and learn how to fish for people.

John's name means "the grace or mercy of the Lord." His family, the Zebedees, were likely an upper middle class family in the Galilee fishing industry because Scripture states that they employed servants (Mark 1:20). He is often described as being the opposite of Peter—a gentle, quiet, loving disciple.

Peter and John were another couple of risk-takers. As they were minding their own business walking to the 3:00 prayer service at the temple, an opportunity for risk came their way. A lame beggar approached them, and though he had been lame since birth, the two disciples healed him in the name of Jesus.

The newly healed man began to jump, run, dance, and praise God, which, as you can imagine, attracted a huge crowd. Peter and John took the opportunity to share the story of Jesus with the crowd and offered the man as proof of Jesus' message. The healing was an act of compassion and power, but the preaching was a risk.

"Now as they were speaking to the people, the priests, the commander of the temple guard, and the Sadducees confronted them, because they were provoked that they were teaching the people and proclaiming in the person of Jesus the resurrection from the dead. So they seized them and put them in custody until the next day, since it was already evening" (Acts 4:1-3).

Peter and John were arrested for their boldness, but their risk resulted in at least 5,000 people believing in Christ.

Are there any similarities between these stories? What are the differences?

Can you think of any other risks that these men took in their lives?

Have you ever done something risky for God? What was the result?

BURIED TALENT

We don't tend to think of risk in spiritual terms, but risk is one dimension of righteousness. In Matthew 25, Jesus described the kingdom of heaven in terms of risk:

"For it is just like a man going on a journey. He called his own slaves and turned over his possessions to them. To one he gave five talents; to another, two; and to another, one—to each according to his own ability. Then he went on a journey. Immediately the man who had received five talents went, put them to work, and earned five more. In the same way the man with two earned two more. But the man who had received one talent went off, dug a hole in the ground, and hid his master's money" (Matthew 25:14-18).

To fully appreciate this parable, we have to realize that one talent was the ancient equivalent of 20 years of a day-laborer's salary. I don't know about you, but if someone gave me 100 years' wages, I don't know if I would ever take another risk. I would have enough money to last the rest of my life; it would be tempting to play it safe. The servant had more to lose, but he also had more to gain.

Let's continue reading the story:

"After a long time the master of those slaves came and settled accounts with them. The man who had received five talents approached, presented five more talents, and said, 'Master, you gave me five talents. Look, I've earned five more talents.'

"His master said to him, 'Well done, good and faithful slave! You were faithful over a few things; I will put you in charge of many things. Share your master's joy!'" (Matthew 25:19-21).

Let's stop right there and consider how Jesus defined faithfulness. According to this parable, an essential element of faithfulness is risk. I think we tend to think of faithfulness in maintenance terms—holding down the fort and maintaining the status quo. We think that faithfulness is hanging on to what you have. But nothing could be further from the truth. Faithfulness is ROI—return on investment. Faithfulness is multiplying what you have to the best of your God-given ability. Faithfulness isn't minimizing risk; faithfulness is maximizing risk in order to maximize reward.

Given your reading of this parable in Scripture, write your own definition of faithfulness.

If faithfulness means maximizing risks, how faithful are you?

Think about people who you would consider faithful. Have they taken risks? What were they?

For further discussion of developing a lifestyle of risk, check out the video "Take the Plunge" at *chasethelion.com/guide/taking-risks.*

I'm concerned that too many of us have a savings mindset; we want to keep what we have. We're playing not to lose. But the parable of the talents is all about an investment mindset—risking what you have to get more. It's playing to win.

"Then the man who had received one talent also approached and said, 'Master, I know you. You're a difficult man, reaping where you haven't sown and gathering where you haven't scattered seed. So I was afraid and went off and hid your talent in the ground. Look, you have what is yours.'

"But his master replied to him, 'You evil, lazy slave! If you knew that I reap where I haven't sown and gather where I haven't scattered, then you should have deposited my money with the bankers. And when I returned I would have received my money back with interest.

"'So take the talent from him and give it to the one who has 10 talents. For to everyone who has, more will be given, and he will have more than enough. But from the one who does not have, even what he has will be taken away from him. And throw this good-for-nothing slave into the outer darkness. In that place there will be weeping and gnashing of teeth'" (Matthew 25:24-30).

These are some of the harshest words in the Gospels, and they were spoken to someone who broke even. Evidently, breaking even isn't good enough. In the context of this parable, wickedness is equivalent to burying your talent in the ground. It is the byproduct of the fear of loss.

How do Jesus' words strike you? How do they make you feel?

What talents has God given you?

How are you currently investing your talents? Are they safe investments or risky investments?

If you're curious about what else made Ted's list, check out *ted.aol.com*.

What are some other areas where you could invest your talents?

PLAY OFFENSE

A few months ago I read a fascinating story about Ted Leonsis, the owner of the Washington Capitals. Let me pull a Paul Harvey and tell you the story behind the story.

Leonsis made his fortune as an executive at AOL, and he is highly regarded as an entrepreneur and philanthropist. However, if you want to really appreciate who he is and how he got there, you have to hit the rewind button and go back to 1983. At the age of 25, Ted Leonsis was on an Eastern Airlines flight that lost its ability to use its wing flaps and landing gear. The flight attendants cleared the overhead bins, shifted passengers, and gave them a crash course in crash landings.

Meanwhile Ted Leonsis began to think about what he would do if he survived. He says, "I promised myself that if I didn't die, I'd play offense for the rest of my life." Leonsis survived the landing and compiled a list of 101 things he wanted to do. To date, he has accomplished 74 of those 101 things. He came up with categories like family matters, financial issues, travel, and charities, and he started setting goals. Here are some of the goals he has accomplished to date:[1]

1) Fall in love and get married.

14) Gain a worth of $100 million, after taxes.

22) Create the world's largest media company.

24) Own a jet.

35) Give $1 million to Georgetown University.

37) Start a family foundation.

40) Own a sports franchise.

83) Produce a TV show.

86) Invent a board game.

92) Hold elective office.

I love those life goals, but I love the motivation behind them even more. Leonsis has a simple mission statement: play offense with your life.

Satan wants us to live in a defensive posture, and he uses two primary tactics to accomplish it—fear and discouragement. He wants us to run away from fear, uncertainty, and risk. But Christ calls us to chase lions. Satan would love nothing more than for our ultimate goal to be to avoid sin. However, doing nothing wrong doesn't constitute doing something right. Goodness is not the absence of badness. Consider the offensive posture described throughout Scripture:

"Put on the full armor of God so that you can stand against the tactics of the Devil" (Ephesians 6:11).

"... put on the new man, the one created according to God's [likeness] in righteousness and purity of the truth.

"Since you put away lying, Speak the truth, each one to his neighbor, because we are members of one another. Be angry and do not sin. Don't let the sun go down on your anger, and don't give the Devil an opportunity. The thief must no longer steal. Instead, he must do honest work with his own hands, so that he has something to share with anyone in need" (Ephesians 4:24-28).

List 10 life goals (risks).

What is tempting about living life defensively?

What areas of your life do you live offensively?

Block out some time for a viewing of *Schlinder's List*. Can one risk-taker really make a difference in the world?

INACTION REGRETS

In his book, *If Only*, psychologist Dr. Neil Roese makes a distinction between two different types of regret: regrets of action and regrets of inaction. A regret of action is doing something you wish you hadn't done. A regret of inaction is not doing something that you wish you had done. In theological terms, action regrets are the result of sins of commission while inaction regrets are the result of sins of omission.

I think the church has fixated on sins of commission long enough. They may be easier to quantify, but the greatest regrets at the end of our lives won't be the things we did wrong. Our greatest regrets will be not having done the right things—things we could have, should have, and would have done.

What is a sin of omission that you need to confess?

List three things you can do this week to reverse this sin of omission in your life.

Action regrets taste bad, but inaction regrets leave a bitter aftertaste that lasts a lifetime. They haunt us because they leave us asking 'what if?'. *What if we had chased the lion instead of running away?*

Somehow our lives seem incomplete. Failing to take a risk is almost like losing a piece of the jigsaw puzzle to your life—it leaves a gaping hole. When we get to the end of our lives, our greatest regrets will be the missing pieces.

That conviction is backed up by the research of two social psychologists named Tom Gilovich and Vicki Medvec. Their research found that time is a key factor in what we regret. Over the short term, we tend to regret our actions. But over the long haul, we tend to regret our inactions. Their study found that over the course of an average week, action regrets outnumber inaction regrets 53 percent to 47 percent. But when people look at their lives as a whole, inaction regrets outnumber action regrets 84 percent to 16 percent.[2]

In other words, our greatest regret at the end of our lives will be the lions we didn't chase.

RUN

We are going to take some risks together in this study. To be a risk-taker, we must have a risk-taker's mind and a risk-taker's heart. To be thoroughly equipped as a lion-chaser, you must train yourself mentally and spiritually. This comes through Scripture memorization and prayer.

Each week, you will be given a Scripture to memorize and a prayer experiment to try. As you participate in these exercises, you will start to see the heart of a lion-chaser beginning to form inside of you. Think of them as marching orders—a battle plan to engage the lions around you.

MENTAL PREPARATION:
SCRIPTURE MEMORY

"And Jesus replied, 'I assure you that when I, the Son of Man, sit upon my glorious throne in the Kingdom, you who have been my followers will also sit on twelve thrones, judging the twelve tribes of Israel. And everyone who has given up houses or brothers or sisters or father or mother or children or property, for my sake, will receive a hundred times as much in return and will have eternal life'" (Matthew 19:28-30, NIV).

SPIRITUAL PREPARATION:
PRAYER EXPERIMENT

Risk-taking is fostered by a vibrant prayer life. When you pray, are you primarily concerned about asking for the strength to serve God's purposes or about asking God to serve your purposes? For this week's prayer experiment, write out a risk-taker's prayer. Include the following:

- Ask God to give you the courage and heart of a risk-taker.

- Confess any sins of omission.

- Ask God if there are any risks He wants you to take. Listen.

- Specifically write out one risky request (examples: Ask God to give you an opportunity to share your faith with someone, befriend someone who isn't like you, serve your community, go on a mission trip, turn in your resignation, send in your résumé, etc.).

- Thank God for allowing you to be a part of His adventure.

NOTES

NOTES

seize *{verb}*: to possess or take by force; capture

opportunity *{noun}*: a good chance for advancement or progress

RECENTLY, A FRIEND OF MINE SENT ME A STARBUCKS GIFT CARD. It wasn't just any Starbucks gift card. It was an Australian Starbucks gift card. I guess different countries have different gift cards, so my friend got one and sent it to me. I couldn't help but think about what a worldwide phenomenon this coffee shop from the Northwest has become. It's synonymous with coffee and coffeehouses. There seems to be a Starbucks on every street corner, in every terminal, in every mall, and in every hotel in the United States.

I love the Starbucks history.

When Howard Schultz purchased Starbucks on August 15, 1987, it was a small chain of coffeehouses in Seattle, Washington. Nothing more; nothing less. Howard Schultz said his earth-shattering, mind-blowing goal at that time was to open a store in Portland, Oregon. A few decades later, there are 11,000 stores in 37 countries with approximately 35 million customer visits every week! And for what it's worth, Starbucks opens five new stores every day, 365 days a year.

SEIZING OPPORTUNITIES

SESSION TWO

CARPE COFFEE

Howard Schultz almost passed up the opportunity to purchase Starbucks because it seemed too big. Schultz said it felt like a case of the salmon swallowing the whale. In other words, it seemed like a 500-pound lion. The asking price was $4 million. I love the way Schultz describes that moment:

"This is my moment, I thought. If I don't seize the opportunity, if I don't step out of my comfort zone and risk it all, if I let too much time tick on, my moment will pass. I knew that if I didn't take advantage of this opportunity, I would replay it in my mind for my whole life, wondering: What if?"[3]

On June 26, 1992—less than five years after Howard Schultz seized the opportunity—Starbucks' stock went public. It was the second most active stock traded on the NASDAQ, and by the closing bell, its market capitalization stood at $273 million. Not bad for a $4 million investment.

Schultz saw an opportunity, and he seized it.

> List people you know who have seized opportunities. Were they encouraged or discouraged by the people around them? What was the outcome?

> What opportunities have you seized in your own life? Are there any opportunities you wish you had seized?

ETYMOLOGY OF OPPORTUNITY

Nestled into Colossians 4, there's a verse that doesn't get much air time, but I think of it as a great definition of spiritual maturity. If all of us obeyed this verse, it would revolutionize our lives.

You can check out the full Howard Schultz story in his autobiography, *Pour Your Heart Into It.*

"Make the most of every opportunity" (Colossians 4:5, NIV).

This Scripture doesn't specify how many or how few opportunities. It doesn't quantify how small or how large the opportunity. We simply need to make the most of every opportunity.

Seeing and seizing opportunities is an underappreciated dimension of spiritual maturity. We are surrounded by God-ordained opportunities— opportunities to love, to laugh, to give, to learn, and to serve. Seeing and seizing those opportunities is at the heart of what it means to follow Christ and be filled with His Spirit.

Now here's the catch: The old aphorism is wrong. Opportunity doesn't knock. The giant Egyptian that Benaiah battled didn't knock *on* the door; he knocked *down* the door. And the lion didn't roll over and play dead. Opportunity roars!

Most of us want our opportunities gift wrapped. We want our lions stuffed or caged or cooked medium well and served on a silver platter. But opportunities typically present themselves at the most inopportune times and in the most inopportune places. Opportunities often come disguised as big, hairy, audacious problems, but lion-chasers don't see problems. They see 500-pound opportunities!

I love the way the Chinese language captures the two sides of this truth. The word "crisis" is made up of two characters—one means danger and the other means opportunity.

Problems are opportunities in disguise.

> Had you ever considered that a dimension of spiritual maturity is the ability to see and seize opportunities? On a scale of 1 to 10, how good are you at seeing opportunities? How good are you at seizing opportunities?

The word translated "opportunity" in Colossians 4:5 is the Greek word *kairos*. It refers to a serendipitous window of opportunity.

Can you think of other biblical examples of people seeing and seizing opportunities?

Describe a time in your life when you turned a potential problem into an opportunity.

What problems are you currently facing that might be opportunities in disguise?

The English word "opportunity" comes from the Latin phrase *ob portu*. In the days before modern harbors, ships had to wait till flood tide to make it into port. The Latin phrase *ob portu* referred to that single moment in time when the tide would turn.

FOR SUCH A TIME AS THIS

I have a conviction: God is in the business of making sure we meet the right people at the right time. He's also in the business of strategically positioning us in the right place at the right time. But here's the catch: The right place often seems like the wrong place, and the right time often seems like the wrong time.

Esther is a classic example.

In the fifth century B.C., King Xerxes ordered the genocide of the Jews. But through an amazing set of circumstances, God used a beauty pageant to strategically position a Jewish orphan girl named Esther as the queen of Persia. No one knew that Esther was Jewish. Not even the king.

So on one level, it seems like Esther was in the wrong place at the wrong time. Look at it from her perspective—your husband has ordered the execution of the Jews. And, unbeknownst to him, you're Jewish. But Esther had a wise uncle named Mordecai who renewed her sense of destiny.

"Mordecai told [the messenger] to reply to Esther, 'Don't think that you will escape the fate of all the Jews because you are in the king's palace. If you keep silent at this time, liberation and deliverance will come to the Jewish people from another place, but you and your father's house will be destroyed. Who knows, perhaps you have come to the kingdom for such a time as this.'

"Esther sent this reply to Mordecai: 'Go and assemble all the Jews who can be found in Susa and fast for me. Don't eat or drink for three days, night and day. I and my female servants will also fast in the same way. After that, I will go to the king even if it is against the law. If I perish, I perish'" (Esther 4:13-16).

According to Persian law, no one could approach the king unless they were summoned—not even his wife. The penalty was death. The only exception was if the king raised his scepter as a symbol to spare the life of the one who had approached him. If you read the first chapter of Esther, you'll find that Xerxes had already gotten rid of one wife who didn't come when he called her. What would keep him from doing the same to a wife that came when he hadn't called her?

I think this situation qualified as a crisis. The genocide of the Jews was a serious problem, but prayer has a way of turning problems into opportunities. To borrow the phrase from Latin, three days of praying and fasting will *ob portu*—it will turn the tide!

To make a long story short, the man who instigated this genocide ended up being killed on the very gallows he built—poetic justice. Not only did Xerxes give the traitor's estate to Esther, but he gave his signet ring to Mordecai, elevating Mordecai to a position of power that only hours before would have been unthinkable.

Go back and read the entire story of Esther for the finer points. What opportunity was presented to Esther?

What was the opposition, the risk, and the potential reward?

The consensus among historians is that Xerxes was impulsive and unpredictable. During his reign, Xerxes commissioned the building of a bridge, but during construction, it was destroyed by a storm. Xerxes ordered that the body of water receive 300 lashes, and he had the bridge builders beheaded.

List the other people who played a role in this story. Did they encourage or discourage Esther from seizing her opportunity?

Is there someone in your life who needs to be encouraged to seize an opportunity?

List their name and one practical thing you can do this week to encourage them.

PRAYER MODE

Colossians 4:5 says, "Make the most of every opportunity" (NIV). How do we do that? I think the answer is found in verse 2:

"Devote yourselves to prayer, being watchful and thankful" (NIV).

The word "watchful" is a throwback to the Old Testament watchmen whose job was to sit on the city wall, scan the horizon, and keep watch. They were the first ones to see an attacking army or traveling traders. People who live in prayer mode are watchmen. They see further than others see. They always see things before others see them and, sometimes, they see things other people *don't* see.

I honestly think that there are only two ways to live your life—survival mode or prayer mode. Survival mode is simply reacting to the circumstances around you.

If Esther had been in survival mode, I think she would have tried to conceal her identity and save herself. But three days of prayer and fasting gave her the moral courage to appeal to the king.

If Benaiah had been in survival mode, he never would have chased the lion. He would have run away.

Survival mode is reactive; prayer mode is proactive.

In prayer mode, your spiritual antenna is up, and your radar is on. Prayer puts you in a proactive posture. In fact, the Aramaic word for prayer, *slotha*, means to set a trap. In other words, prayer helps us catch the opportunities that cross our paths. People who live in prayer mode see opportunities that other people don't even notice. People who don't live in prayer mode are opportunity blind.

All I know is this: When I pray, providence happens. In this sense, prayer is not just an end in itself. It is a means to an end, and the end goal is seeing and seizing opportunities.

In what areas of your life do you tend to live in survival mode?

In what areas of your life do you tend to live in prayer mode?

Richard Foster is recognized as a leader in the development of Christian disciplines. Listen to a podcast based on his book *Prayer* at *podcast. christianaudio.com*.

After reading the definition for the Aramaic word for prayer, do you view prayer any differently? If so, how?

What are some practical things you can do to move toward prayer mode living?

What are some prayer traps that you need to set?

THE RETICULAR ACTIVATING SYSTEM

Let's look at one passage on prayer and then try to put prayer into a neurological context.

Psalm 5:3 reveals the way David started every day. It was part of his morning ritual.

"At daybreak, LORD, You hear my voice; at daybreak I plead my case to You and watch expectantly."

One of our greatest spiritual shortcomings is low expectations. We don't expect much from God because we aren't asking for much. When my prayer life is firing on all eight cylinders, I can believe God for everything. However, when I'm in a prayer slump, I have a hard time believing God for anything. Low expectations are the byproduct of prayerlessness, but prayer has a way of God-sizing our expectations. David couldn't wait to see what God was going to do next because he was living in prayer mode. The more you pray, the higher your expectations.

So prayer sanctifies our expectations, but it also creates cognitive categories in our reticular activating system.

Let me explain . . .

At the base of our brain stem, there is a cluster of nerve cells called the reticular activating system (RAS). Our brains are bombarded by stimuli all the time—sights, sounds, and smells. If we had to process or pay attention to all the stimuli, it would drive us crazy. The RAS determines what gets noticed and what goes unnoticed. Think of it as your mental radar system.

Here's how it works: When you purchase a cell phone or clothing or a car, a category in your reticular activating system is created. Suddenly you notice if someone's cell phone has the same ring tone don't you? You mistakenly try to answer yours. You notice if someone is wearing your outfit at the same event. Can you say awkward? And the second you drive your new car out of the lot, it seems like everyone is driving your model of car.

Listen to the audio file "Moving Out." Your group leader will send it to you via e-mail. Is there an opportunity in your life to seize? What's holding you back?

That is the function of the RAS. You didn't have a category for your ring tone or clothing or car before you bought it. But once you downloaded the ring tone or made the purchase or drove out of the dealership, you had a new cognitive category.

So what does that have to do with prayer?

When we pray for someone or something, it creates a category in our reticular activating system. Prayer is important for the same reason goals are important. We need to create categories so we will notice anything and everything that God does to answer those prayers or achieve those goals.

If you want to see and seize God-ordained opportunities, you've got to live in prayer mode. You've got to lay your requests before the Lord.

Do you pray better in the morning, the middle of the day, or at night? Do you think that praying in the morning is important?

How is your current prayer life affecting your expectations?

THE GREATEST OPPORTUNITY

Spiritual maturity is all about seeing and seizing opportunities. That is how our spiritual journey begins. It begins by seizing the greatest opportunity we'll ever be offered—the opportunity to spend eternity with God. John 1:12 says:

"But to all who did receive Him, He gave them the right to be children of God."

All we have to do to seize the opportunity is receive Christ. In a sense, we agree to a set of terms. The terms are spelled out in 2 Corinthians 5:21:

"[God] made the One who did not know sin to be sin for us, so that we might become the righteousness of God in Him."

So here's the deal. It's like God says, "Let's take everything you've ever done wrong—all of your spiritual debits—and transfer them to my account. Then, let's take everything Jesus did right—all of His spiritual credits—and transfer them to your account. And then we'll call it even."

What a deal. The way we receive Christ is by accepting the offer that is on the table. We simply put our faith in who Christ is and what Christ has done.

We seal the deal via faith.

Why wait? Seize the opportunity.

Carpe Christ.

> Have you ever seized the opportunity that Christ has offered to us? If so, list three ways in which Christ has made a difference in your life. If not, consider asking your small group leader more about this opportunity.

MENTAL PREPARATION:
SCRIPTURE MEMORY

"Be very careful, then, how you live—not as unwise but as wise, making the most of every opportunity, because the days are evil" (Ephesians 5:15-16, NIV).

SPIRITUAL PREPARATION:
PRAYER EXPERIMENT

Over the next week, begin each day by praying the following:

"At daybreak, Lord, You hear my voice; at daybreak,
I plead my case to You and watch expectantly" (Psalm 5:3).

- After praying that verse, spend one minute in silence, meditating on God and His provision in your life.

- Make a list of the things you are thankful for.

- Make a list of the things you are prayerfully expecting God to do.

- Over the course of the week, does your list change any? If so, how?

NOTES

NOTES

face *{verb}*: to confront impudently

fear *{noun}*: an unpleasant often strong emotion caused by anticipation of danger

IT IS SO EASY TO READ about a lion encounter that happened 3,000 years ago and totally underestimate the fear factor. I wonder if Benaiah suffered from post-traumatic stress syndrome. Sure, he killed the lion, but not before it scared the living daylights out of him. He was inches from 30 bared teeth. I don't think he ever forgot the smell of the lion's bloody breath, and the sound of the roar had to echo in his mind's ear forever.

I don't care how battle-tested or battle-scarred you are. I don't care how crazy or courageous you are. You don't come face-to-face with a 500-pound lion without experiencing sheer terror. But one thing sets lion-chasers apart—they don't run away from the things that scare them. Normal people don't chase lions, but lion chasers aren't normal.

Lion-chasers chase their fears.

FACING FEARS
SESSION THREE

FEAR FACTOR

If you consider this story at face value, it has to be one of the most improbable reactions recorded in Scripture, as counterintuitive as you can get. The natural reaction when the image of a lion travels through the optic nerve into the visual cortex is to run away as fast and as far as you can. Benaiah had the opposite reaction. As improbable as falling up or the secondhand on your watch moving counterclockwise, the lion ran away as Benaiah gave chase.

Hold that thought.

> How do you react to fears—do you chase them or do they chase you?

> List three fears you are currently facing. How are you responding to them—running from them, ignoring them, or chasing them?

Listen to "Faith Enough" by Jars of Clay. What role does your faith currently play in your reaction to fear?

CONDITIONED REFLEX

At the turn of the last century, a Russian psychologist and physician named Ivan Pavlov did some experiments with dogs that made him famous. In fact, he won a Nobel Prize.

Pavlov wanted to find out how conditioned reflexes were acquired. He knew that dogs naturally salivate over food, but he wanted to see if salivation could be caused by another stimulus. Pavlov discovered that if he rang a bell before feeding the dogs that eventually the ringing bell would cause salivation even without the food. Pavlov referred to this learned relationship as a "conditioned reflex." The discovery is actually a restatement of what Aristotle referred to as the law of congruity: "When two things commonly occur together, the appearance of one will bring the other to mind." That is the way God has wired the human mind.

What I want you to see is that all of us have been conditioned a lot more than we realize. To one degree or another, all of us are Pavlovian. Over the course of our lifetimes, we both consciously and subconsciously acquire an elaborate set of conditioned reflexes—some good and some bad. Let me give you an example.

Every time I fill up with a tank of gas, I look out my rearview mirror to make sure the hose isn't still in the car. Anybody want to take a wild guess why? Because I didn't look in the rearview mirror a few years ago, I pulled the hose right out of the gas pump. Imagine a car with a tail. That's what it looked like as I drove away from the pump. Every time I pull away, I imagine that I forgot to take the hose out. It's a conditioned reflex. Now here is the trick.

Those conditioned reflexes can be good or bad. I think the conviction of the Holy Spirit when we sin is a healthy and holy conditioned reflex. Many of us, however, have another conditioned reflex that is neither holy nor healthy—that of false guilt. Some of us feel guilty over confessed sin, and we shouldn't. God has forgiven and forgotten. It's harder for us to forgive because we can't forget.

ROOSTER'S CROW

If you look at Scripture through the filter of Ivan Pavlov, there are some fascinating conditioned reflexes. All four Gospels record the story of Peter denying Christ. Luke 22:60 says that right as Peter was denying Christ the third time, a rooster crowed.

At that moment, the Lord turned and looked straight at Peter. Then Peter remembered the word the Lord had spoken to him: "Before the rooster crows today, you will deny Me three times." And Peter went outside and wept bitterly.

This had to be the most painful failure of Peter's life. I have to wonder if Peter felt a twinge of guilt every time a rooster crowed. You know how certain stimuli trigger certain memories? A sight or sound or smell can unlock memories that we thought we had forgotten. I think that the sound of a rooster crowing must have had a physiological effect that produced feelings of guilt in Peter.

Imagine what it was like for Peter every morning. It was a daily reminder of his failure. The rooster's crow was a stimulus, just like Pavlov's ringing bell.

Now, let me tell you what the enemy wants to do. Satan wants to remind you of your worst failures over and over and over again. He wants to crow like a rooster every morning.

While Jesus calls us to be revolutionaries, Satan wants to turn us into reactionaries. He wants to condition our reflexes with guilt and fear. Jesus came to recondition our reflexes.

Instead of hating our enemies, we pray for those who persecute us. Instead of trying to be first, we go last. Jesus said that whoever keeps his life will lose it and whoever loses his life will keep it. When we get slapped on the cheek, we don't slap back; we turn the other one.

For what it's worth, I think it's easy to *act like* a Christian. It is much more difficult to *react like* a Christian.

> **Do you agree? What is the difference? Which one is easier for you?**

> **Describe a time in your life during the past week when it was difficult to react like a Christian.**

RECONDITIONED BY GRACE

Now fast-forward to John 21. Post-denial Peter told the other disciples, "I'm going out to fish." I suppose it's possible that Peter just wanted to go fishing, but part of me wonders if Peter thought his career as a disciple was over. Perhaps he thought he had failed one too many times, so he was going back to his former life. There is nothing that Satan would have loved more than for Peter to spend the rest of his life fishing in a boat on the Sea of Galilee instead of going to the ends of the earth fulfilling the Great Commission.

As I said, Satan wants to neutralize us. But Jesus reconditioned Peter in a profound way. In a sense, He reinstated Peter three times. Three times he asked Peter: "Do you love Me?" Peter must have been a little offended by the third time, so why did Jesus ask three times? Maybe Jesus knew about conditioned reflexes long before Pavlov did his experiments. And Jesus did what He does so well—He took that guilt and reconditioned it with grace.

One last observation. Interestingly enough, John 21:4 says that Peter's encounter with Jesus was early in the morning. When do roosters crow?

I think Jesus reconditioned Peter so that the sound of a rooster's crow was no longer a reminder of his guilt—it was a daily reminder of God's grace. The enemy wants to remind you of your worst failures. Maybe you need to be reminded that the grace of God is much bigger than your worst failure. I love what F. Scott Fitzgerald said: "Never confuse a single mistake with a final mistake."

The grace of God turns final mistakes into single mistakes.

I'm impressed with the people in the Gospels who put their faith in Christ, but it is even more remarkable to me that Jesus put His faith in the people that He did. Peter messed up, but Jesus didn't give up. God wants to recondition our guilt with grace, and He wants to recondition our fear with faith.

In John 21, two words for "love" are used. Jesus asked Peter for the *agape* kind of love—that is, perfect, God-like love. Peter responded that He loved Jesus with the *phileo* kind of love. That love is more of a friendship or brotherly kind of love.

> Describe a time in your life when God extended grace to you after you'd done something to disappoint Him.

> Read John 21:15-17. What action items did Jesus give to Peter? Why do you think He followed His questions with these action steps?

> Is there any guilt in your life that needs to be reconditioned with grace? List it here and pause to ask God to trade that guilt for His grace.

Are there fears in your life that need to be reconditioned by faith? List them here and pause to ask God to trade that fear for faith.

UNLEARNING

Jesus' famous Sermon on the Mount can be found in Matthew 5-7. When Jesus referred to "the law and the prophets," He meant the entire Old Testament. The Pharisees had created 248 commandments and 365 prohibitions based on the Old Testament law.

Half of learning is learning, but the other half of learning is *unlearning*. Unfortunately, unlearning is twice as hard as learning. It's like missing your exit on the freeway—you have to drive to the next exit and then double back. Every mile you go in the wrong direction is really a two-mile error. Unlearning is twice as hard, and it often takes twice as long. It's harder to get old thoughts out of your mind than it is to get new thoughts into your mind. That's the challenge Jesus faced, isn't it? If you study the teachings of Christ, you'll realize that learning wasn't His primary goal. His primary goal was unlearning. He was reverse-engineering religious minds, and those can be the toughest minds to change. That's why two phrases are repeated over and over again in the Sermon on the Mount.

"You have heard that it was said . . . "

"But I tell you . . . "

What was Jesus saying and doing? He was uninstalling religious assumptions and upgrading them with spiritual truths.

"You have heard that it was said, 'An eye for eye, and a tooth for a tooth.' But I tell you, don't resist an evildoer. On the contrary, if anyone slaps you on your right cheek, turn the other to him also" (Matthew 5:38-39).

"You have heard that it was said, 'Do not commit adultery.' But I tell you everyone who looks at a woman to lust for her has already committed adultery with her in his heart" (Matthew 5:27-28).

"You have heard that it was said, 'Love your neighbor and hate your enemy.' But I tell you, love your enemies and pray for those who persecute you" (Matthew 5:43-44).

What were the Old Testament concepts in these verses? What were Jesus' new teachings? How can we apply this in our lives?

The sermon contains the Beatitudes (Matthew 5:3-11), the Lord's Prayer (Matthew 6:9-13), and the Golden Rule (Matthew 7:12). It seems to be Jesus' commentary on the Ten Commandments.

Half of spiritual growth is learning what we don't know. The other half is unlearning what we do. Our failure to unlearn irrational fears and misconceptions keeps us from becoming who God wants us to be.

The invalid in John 5:1-9 is a great example of the importance of unlearning. He had been crippled for 38 years when Jesus asked him if he wanted to get well. The man believed there was only one way to be healed: "I don't have a man to put me into the pool when the water is stirred up, but while I'm coming, someone goes down ahead of me." This man made an assumption that may have cost him almost four decades!

He only had one category for healing. He assumed, based on ancient superstition, that he had to be the first one into the pool of Bethesda when the water was stirred in order to be healed. In a sense, he was imprisoned by what he knew. Jesus uninstalled that mistaken belief with one sentence: "Get up, pick up your bedroll and walk!"

Notice that Jesus didn't just set this man free physically—He set him free cognitively. Faith is unlearning the senseless worries and misguided beliefs that hold us captive. It's far more complex than simply modifying behavior. Faith involves synaptogenesis. Faith is rewiring the human brain. Neurologically speaking, that is what we do when we study Scripture. We are literally upgrading our minds by downloading the mind of Christ.

The pool of Bethesda (house of grace) was located on the eastern side of Jerusalem near the Temple Mount and the Sheep Gate (referenced in Nehemiah 3:1) and was fed by a nearby spring.

Jesus healed the lame man in an unexpected way that went against the prevailing religious understanding. Have you ever seen God work in your life or in someone else's life in a way that was different from your religions expectations? What happened?

Can you think of other instances in Scripture when Jesus did something that was outside the box of religion's rules or expectations? Look for three examples in the New Testament and list them below.

"Do not conform to this age, but be transformed by the renewing of your mind" (Romans 12:2a).

Just as a computer hard drive needs to be defragmented to optimize performance, our minds need to be defragmented. So how do we defragment our faith? How do we renew our minds? How do we get ourselves out of the mental pit we've gotten ourselves into? We upgrade our minds by downloading Scripture.

What is the relationship between memorizing Scripture and facing your fears?

Listen to the audio file "Digging In." Your group leader will send it to you via e-mail. Has fear held you back from following through on opportunities in the past?

BATTER'S BOX

When I was a little kid I played little league baseball, and I definitely have some good memories. I hit a few home runs and made a few all-star teams. I also have a few bad memories.

My most memorable moment was getting hit by a pitch during a little league game. I was actually knocked unconscious for a few moments, but I remember everything about it. I remember a crowd of people hovering over me. I remember being lifted into the ambulance and rushed to the hospital. I remember them putting those EKG patches on me to do some tests.

Now, what do you think was going through my head the next time I stepped into the batter's box? The next at bat was the toughest of my life because, subconsciously, I was afraid that what happened before was going to happen again. My coach would yell, "Keep your head in there," but my head would yell back, "It's not *your* head in here!" I had a conditioned reflex. Every time a pitch was high and inside, I felt like backing out of the batter's box.

I had a choice to make. I could stop playing the game and forfeit all that fun, or I could face my fear and step into the batter's box. I wish I could say that I hit a home run my next at bat, but I honestly don't remember. I'm glad I don't because courage has nothing to do with whether or not you hit a home run or strike out. Courage is getting back into the batter's box.

FACING YOUR FEARS

It's tough to get back into the batter's box after you've been hit by a pitch relationally.

Maybe you struggle with the fear of intimacy because you got really close to someone and then got hurt. You need to get back into the batter's box. After all, if you don't get back in the game relationally, you'll never get to first base!

Maybe it's the fear of rejection—a rejection letter from an employer or school. Believe me, I had to take it on the chin from a lot of publishers. I had to get back in the box if I ever wanted people to read what I wanted to write.

Maybe it's the fear of failure. When I was in seminary, we tried to plant a church. We formed a core group. We had a bank account. We had a name. One minor detail was missing—we never had a service. The church never even got off the ground. I felt like a failure. That failure could have kept me out of the batter's box, but it's hard to imagine forfeiting the church that I'm a part of now.

Don't let your fears and failures keep you out of the batter's box. Maybe it's time to get back into the batter's box and swing for the fences.

> Are there any "batter's boxes" in your life that you need to step back into? What are they? What is one practical thing you can do next week to step back into the batter's box?

A LIFE WORTH TELLING STORIES ABOUT

Don't let mental lions keep you from experiencing everything God has to offer. The greatest opportunities will often double as the scariest experiences. The defining moments will often double as the scariest decisions.

In the words of David Whyte: "The price of our vitality is the sum of our fears."

Benaiah must have been scared spitless when he encountered that lion, but he didn't run away. Evidently, faith had reconditioned his fear because he chased the lion, and it was the fear he felt that made his lion story all the more fun to tell ex post facto.

Imagine the bedtime stories Benaiah must have told his children. I can hear his kids: "Tell us the lion story one more time!" I think we owe it to our kids and grandkids to live our lives in a way that is worth telling stories about. And more importantly, we owe it to God.

So here is my question: Are you living your life in a way that is worth telling stories about?

Maybe it is time to quit running and start chasing.

> **What are the messages of the stories of your life? Are they stories worth telling?**

ACCUMULATE EXPERIENCES

Jesus issued a challenged to the rich young ruler in Matthew 19:21:

"If you want to be perfect, go, sell your belongings and give to the poor, and you will have treasure in heaven. Then come, follow Me."

> When you read Jesus' command to the rich young ruler, what impacts you most: the command to give everything up or the opportunity to follow Christ?

I think you can read this challenge two ways. From one perspective, Jesus was asking this man to sacrifice everything. He told him to give everything away. From another perspective, he offered this 20-something the opportunity of a lifetime. He offered him an apprenticeship with the Son of God.

What dollar value would you put on that kind of experience? You've got to admit that an internship with the Son of God looks awfully good on a résumé.

Most people would give anything to get close to greatness. What golfer wouldn't love to caddie for Tiger Woods for 18 holes? What movie buff wouldn't love to be Steven Spielberg's sidekick during the production of a blockbuster? What entrepreneur wouldn't love an opportunity to be Donald Trump's apprentice? Can I point something out?

Jesus took a group of uneducated fishermen and turned them into history-makers and world-changers. In a day and age when the average person never traveled outside a 30-mile radius of their home, Jesus told them to "go into all the world." This was 1,500 years before the age of exploration. Talk about adventure!

These fishermen, who grew up and lived their whole lives within a stone's throw of the Sea of Galilee, traveled all over the ancient world and turned the world upside down. According to Eusebius, Peter went to Italy. John ended up in Asia. James the son of Zebedee ended up in Spain. Even "doubting" Thomas got out of the boat and ventured to India.

Think about all that they experienced during their time with Christ. They had box seats to every sermon Jesus preached and every miracle Jesus performed. They were with Him night and day. They literally got to share an office with the Son of God.

The disciples were poor in terms of material possessions, but they accumulated a wealth of experience. I think this rich young ruler had it backward—he forfeited a wealth of experience because he was more concerned about accumulating possessions. Now let me cut to the chase: life is not about accumulating material possessions. Your greatest possession isn't your bank account; it's the experiences you accumulate when you get out of the boat and follow Jesus. Life is about accumulating experiences, and those experiences become our priceless possessions.

Eusebius, known as "the Father of Church History," was the bishop of Caesarea in Palestine and lived around 260-341 A.D. You can read his writings in *The History of the Church: From Christ to Constantine* and *Eusebius: The Church History.*

What do you consider to be your greatest possessions?

Up to this point, are your experiences more priceless than your possessions?

Check out an example of facing fear in the short film "Remember the Slide" at *chasethelion.com/guide/facing-fears*.

What are some experiences you would like to have at some point during your life?

CHASE THE LION

Satan wants to scare the living daylights out of you, but you have a choice. You can run away or give chase. First Peter 5:8 pictures Satan as "a roaring lion, looking for anyone he can devour."

This is where *Chase the Lion* becomes a double entendre. There are two places in Scripture where we are told to resist the devil.

One is 1 Peter 5:9: "Resist him, firm in [your] faith . . ." The other is James 4:7: "But resist the Devil, and he will flee from you."

The word "flee" in James 4:7 is the Greek word *phuego,* and it literally means "to run away." God doesn't want us to run away from the enemy; He wants the enemy to run away from us.

God wants to raise up a generation of lion-chasers who don't just run away from evil. He wants a generation of lion-chasers that put the enemy to flight.

Does James 4:7 change your understanding of how we are to react to the enemy? If so, how?

Do you tend to live reactively (running away from the enemy) or proactively (chasing the enemy away from you)?

MENTAL PREPARATION:
SCRIPTURE MEMORY

"Do not conform any longer to the pattern of this world, but be transformed by the renewing of your mind" (Romans 12:2a, NIV).

SPIRITUAL PREPARATION:
PRAYER EXPERIMENT

Too many of us pray as if God's primary objective is to keep us from getting scared. Our prayer lists revolve around the desire to keep us, our families, and our friends safe. But the goal of life is not the elimination of fear. The goal is to muster the moral courage to chase lions.

୧ Write down an area where you need to pray for courage:

୧ Now, write out a lion-chaser prayer about that situation:

NOTES

NOTES

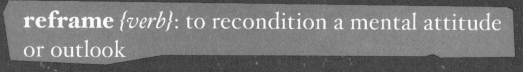

reframe *{verb}*: to recondition a mental attitude or outlook

problem *{noun}*: a source of perplexity, distress or vexation

IN 1994 I GRADUATED FROM SEMINARY in the Chicago area, and my wife Lora and I moved to D.C., to direct a parachurch ministry. One of my students was a man named Charles who was from Nigeria. Charles must have been in his mid-60s, and he walked with a cane and talked with a slur because of a stroke that had affected his speech and motor skills. Sometimes I'd give Charles a ride to or from class, and I had to physically help him get in and out of the car because he couldn't bend his leg. Nothing came easy for Charles.

One day I went to pick Charles up for class. He lived in a public housing tenement—the kind of place you live in only because you can't live any place else. I'll never forget the hat that he was wearing. Maybe it was the juxtaposition that struck me. He could barely walk. He could barely talk. But Charles was wearing a hat that said "God is good."

I was overwhelmed by the conviction of the Holy Spirit, and I thought: *What right do I have to complain about anything?* Anytime I feel like throwing a pity party, I think about Charles.

I think a lot of people going through those kinds of circumstances would have become jaded. Their spirits would shrivel until nothing is left but bitterness or anger or pride. I haven't met too many people with a sweeter spirit or kinder heart than Charles.

REFRAMING PROBLEMS

SESSION FOUR

GOD IS GOOD

What is it that enables someone like Charles to overcome that kind of adversity?

That's what this session is about, and it starts with a simple reminder: who you become is not determined by your circumstances. Rather, the outcome of your life will be determined by your outlook on life.

Our greatest problems aren't circumstantial; our greatest problems are perceptual. When we look at life through the frame of Scripture, we begin to see things the way God sees them, and that is the key to overcoming adversity.

> **Name some people you know who, like Charles, praise God despite their circumstances.**

> **Name some people in Scripture who faced tremendous adversity.**

The film *Cinderella Man* tells the story of one man committed to reframing problems and confronting adversity. Plan a viewing soon.

REFRAMING

Think of the Bible as a frame.

I'm neither an interior decorator, nor the son of an interior decorator, but I know that the framing of a picture determines what people notice in that picture. If you put a brown frame around a picture, it will accentuate the brown colors in the picture. If use a blue frame, it will pull out the blue. The frame determines the focus.

If you want to see yourself the way God sees you, you need to look through the frame of Scripture. If you don't, you'll have identity issues.

You also need to look at other people through the frame of Scripture. When you do, you begin to see them as invaluable and irreplaceable. You begin to love people when they least expect it and least deserve it.

Finally, you need to look at life through the frame of Scripture. When you do, the circumstances of your life will start to look remarkably different.

What are some ways that Scripture can change your perspective on yourself, others, and life?

Let me give you some examples. Take a look at how Scripture reframes persecution, trials, and even death.

"Blessed are you when they insult you and persecute you and falsely say every kind of evil against you because of Me. Be glad and rejoice, because your reward is great in heaven. For that is how they persecuted the prophets who were before you" (Matthew 5:11-12).

Are you facing any sort of persecution right now? If so, how are you responding? Should this verse change your response in any way?

"Consider it a great joy, my brothers, whenever you experience various trials, knowing that the testing of your faith produces endurance. But endurance must do its complete work, so that you may be mature and complete, lacking nothing" (James 1:2-4).

What is the biggest hardship you are currently facing? How does this verse reframe that hardship for you?

Has there ever been a time that God used a trial to develop maturity in your life? What was it, and what did you learn from it?

"Death has been swallowed up in victory. O Death, where is your victory? O Death, where is your sting? Now the sting of death is sin, and the power of sin is the law. But thanks be to God, who gives us the victory through our Lord Jesus Christ!" (1 Corinthians 15:54b-57).

Scripture is all about reframing.

> What situations are you currently facing that need some Scriptural direction or perspective?

I want you to think of Philippians 1:29 as a frame around adversity. Most of us don't like adversity, but if we put a biblical frame around it, we begin to realize that there are some life lessons and character traits that can only be learned and developed via adversity. In fact, adversity expands our capacity to serve God.

"For it has been given to you on Christ's behalf not only to believe in Him, but also to suffer for Him" (Philippians 1:29).

Now let's be brutally honest. If you're anything like me, there are certain passages of Scripture that you sort of wish didn't make the canonical cut. You know they're true, but you wish they weren't in the Bible because they are so hard to swallow and tough to digest. Those are the verses that often provide the greatest spiritual nourishment if we really chew on them.

> What is a verse in Scripture that is tough for you to swallow? Write it down here. Now, name one way you can grow by embracing, believing, and living out this verse.

Philippians 1:29 is one of those verses that's tough to swallow. We like the belief part but don't care too much for the suffering.

What's fascinating is that the word "granted" comes from the Greek word *charizomai* which means "to grant a favor."

To paraphrase this verse, it's almost like God is saying, "Listen, I owe you a favor. So let Me let you suffer."

We tend to see suffering as a necessary evil at best, but Paul called it a divine favor. Here's the thing—there is nothing theoretical about this approach to life. Paul wrote these words from a middle-eastern jail cell.

> Have you ever noticed God's gift of suffering in this verse before? Why does God grant us the favor of suffering? Why is it a favor?

You can discover the original language for yourself using a concordance, an interlinear Bible, and/or a word dictionary. We recommend *Strong's Exhaustive Concordance*, *Vine's Expository Dictionary of New Testament Words*, and *The Complete Word Study Dictionary* by Spiros Zodhiates.

Look at Paul's résumé of adversity:

"I have worked much harder, been in prison more frequently, been flogged more severely, and been exposed to death again and again. Five times I received from the Jews the forty lashes minus one. Three times I was beaten with rods, once I was stoned, three times I was shipwrecked, I spent a night and a day in the open sea, I have been constantly on the move. I have been in danger from rivers, in danger from bandits, in danger from my own countrymen, in danger from Gentiles; in danger in the city, in danger in the country, in danger at sea; and in danger from false brothers.

"I have labored and toiled and have often gone without sleep; I have known hunger and thirst and have often gone without food; I have been cold and naked. Besides everything else I face daily the pressure of my concern for all the churches. Who is weak, and I do not feel weak? Who is led into sin, and I do not inwardly burn? If I must boast, I will boast of the things that show my weakness" (2 Corinthians 11:23b-30, NIV).

In my observation, no one was more used by God than the Apostle Paul. No one experienced more adversity. Do those things have anything to do with each other? I may not want to write it, and you may not want to read it, but God uses adversity to expand our capacity to serve Him.

How does God use our adversity to expand our capacity to serve Him?

What adversities are you currently facing that you want God to reframe?

WORSHIPING

Looking at our lives against the backdrop of Scripture will help us reframe our problems. Worship is another way to reframe our problems. I think there are two basic types of people in the world: complainers and worshipers. Complainers can always find something to complain about, but worshipers can always find something to praise God about.

The story of Paul and Silas in Acts 16 is a great example:

"Then the mob joined in the attack against them, and the chief magistrates stripped off their clothes and ordered them to be beaten with rods. After they had inflicted many blows on them, they threw them in jail, ordering the jailer to keep them securely guarded. Receiving such an order, he put them into the inner prison and secured their feet in the stocks" (Acts 16:22-24).

If I were Paul or Silas I think I'd be emotionally, physically, and spiritually spent. I'd be drained to the last drop and have nothing left to give. I'd probably question God about my circumstances.

Their backs were bleeding from the beating. They were black and blue all over. They'd landed—in stocks—in the maximum security cell.

It just doesn't get much worse than that. That's why the next verse is so amazing:

"About midnight Paul and Silas were praying and singing hymns to God, and the prisoners were listening to them" (Acts 16:25).

The word used to describe the imprisonment of Paul and Silas in Acts 16 is desmoterion meaning "place of bonds." Roman law recognized three different types of imprisonment: custodia publica (public custody), custodia libera (free custody), and custodia militaris (military custody). Custodia publica was the worst kind, as prisoners were thrown into dungeons. This was the type of imprisonment that Paul and Silas experienced at Philippi.

Read the rest of Acts 16. Write down the chain reaction that occurred because Paul and Silas made a decision to worship instead of complain.

Also called "Silvanus" in the Epistles, Silas accompanied Paul and Barnabas to the Council of Jerusalem and then conveyed the decree of the council to the church in Antioch. He was a Roman citizen, an early church leader, and a prophet (Acts 15:32).

Let me share something I've learned from personal experience: When I get into a spiritual or emotional slump, it's usually because I've zoomed in on a problem. I'm fixating on something that's wrong. I'm focused on the wrong thing. Nine times out of ten, the solution is zooming out so I can get some perspective.

How do we zoom out? Let me give you a one word answer: worship.

Worshiping is taking our eyes off of our external circumstances and focusing on God. We stop focusing on what's wrong with us or our circumstances, and we start focusing on what's right with God.

List three things that are right about God that draw you to worship.

Paul and Silas could have zoomed in and complained about their circumstances, but they made a choice to worship God in spite of their external circumstances.

Worship restores spiritual equilibrium, helps you regain your perspective, and enables you to find something right to praise God about even when everything seems to be going wrong.

Worship is zooming out and refocusing on the big picture. It's refocusing on the fact that 2,000 years ago, Jesus died on the cross to pay the penalty for my sin. It's refocusing on the fact that God loves me when I least expect it and least deserve it. It's refocusing on the fact that God is going to get me where God wants me to go. It's refocusing on the fact that I have eternity with God to look forward to in a place where there is no mourning or sorrow or pain.

Worship is refocusing on the fundamentals of our faith. When we choose worship, God restores the joy of our salvation. We regain our spiritual equilibrium.

Is it easy? Absolutely not. Nothing is more difficult than praising God when everything seems to be going wrong. But one of the purest forms of worship is praising God even when you don't feel like it because it shows God that your worship isn't based on circumstances. Worship is based on the character of God.

Worship reframes our circumstances.

Paul gave some priceless advice in Philippians 4:8:

"Finally brothers, whatever is true, whatever is honorable, whatever is just, whatever is pure, whatever is lovely, whatever is commendable—if there is any moral excellence and if there is any praise—dwell on these things."

A worshiper always finds a reason for praise because they're always looking for what is praiseworthy.

The circumstances you complain about become chains that imprison you. Worship is the way out. Stop focusing on what's wrong about you and your circumstances and start focusing on what's right about God.

> **Are there any circumstances that are currently imprisoning you? What are they?**

> **What things have you complained about over the past week? How can you turn those into opportunities to worship?**

> **List 10 things you are thankful for.**

REMODELING

Let me put adversity in biological terms.

In the world of strength training, there is something called the principle of supercompensation. When an athlete is pushed beyond the threshold of pain and exhaustion, the body overcompensates. The more a muscle is broken down, the more it builds back up.

The same is true of our bones. The 206 bones in the body are constantly going through a process called remodeling. They are being broken down by osteoclasts and built back up by osteoblasts. What's interesting is that the process of remodeling is intensified when a bone is broken. Extra osteoblasts help rebuild the bone. And while there is a period of weakness when the bone is more vulnerable to re-injury, the body overcompensates so it actually becomes stronger than it was before the break. Very rarely does a bone break twice in the same place because the bone is thicker and strongerdue to the first break and its healing.

Sometimes God breaks us where we need to be broken. He fractures the pride and lust and anger in our lives, but He does it to remodel us into His image. Once we heal, we end up stronger than we were to begin with. I wish I could tell you that you can get in shape by sitting in a recliner watching football. We would like that because we want to be in shape without the workout. We want to be smart without the homework. We want to be wealthy without the business plan. We want spiritual maturity without spiritual discipline, but it just doesn't work that way.

There is an old axiom—no pain, no gain. I think some of us operate with a slightly different philosophy of life: no pain, no pain. What we discover is that the path of least resistance is the path of least fruitfulness.

The people God uses the most are often the people who have experienced the most adversity.

I think all three encounters recorded in 2 Samuel 23—taking on two Moabite warriors, a giant Egyptian, and a 500-pound lion—could have ended Benaiah's military career. They were make or break moments. Without those adverse conditions, Benaiah would have disappeared from the pages of Scripture. Adversity turned into an opportunity for Benaiah to prove himself as a valiant warrior, and I bet those three adversities earned him a great performance review or year-end bonus.

Listen to "There Goes the Fear" by the Doves. How are you handling the adversity that comes into your life?

No adversity = no opportunity.

When you look through the frame of Scripture, you see that God used adversity to remodel Benaiah. Each trial remodeled Benaiah as one of David's mighty men, captain of David's bodyguard, army commander, and eventually, commander-in-chief of Israel's army. Benaiah's past experiences prepared him for future opportunities.

I don't know what kind of adversity you're facing, but I know that God is in the remodeling business. Instead of being in such a hurry to get out of adverse situations, sometimes we need to make sure we get something out of those adverse situations. God may be honing skills and developing character traits. Honestly, it is adversity that will present you with the greatest opportunity to prove yourself as a parent, a spouse, a friend, a neighbor, and a leader. Adversity is the seedbed of opportunity.

There is a famous speech in the 1949 film, *The Third Man,* written by Orson Welles, that I have learned to love. My apologies in advance to Swiss readers:

"In Italy for 30 years under the Borgias, they had warfare, terror, murder, and bloodshed—but they produced Michelangelo, Leonardo Da Vinci, and the Renaissance. In Switzerland, they had brotherly love, 500 years of democracy and peace, and what did they produce? The cuckoo clock."[4]

I rest my case.

God is in the remodeling business. He cares more about your long-term potential than your short-term comfort. If you let Him, He'll turn past adversities into future opportunities.

You don't have to go looking for adversity—it will find you. When it does, don't run away. If you have the courage to chase the lion into the pit, you may just discover your destiny in the middle of it.

> Often, the pain we have experienced in our past can become another person's blessing. What adversities have you faced that could become ministry opportunities?

MENTAL PREPARATION:
SCRIPTURE MEMORY

"For it has been given to you on Christ's behalf not only to believe in Him, but also to suffer for Him" (Philippians 1:29).

SPIRITUAL PREPARATION:
PRAYER EXPERIMENT

o   A high percentage of our prayers are aimed at problem reduction. Make a list of the problem situations you are currently facing:

o   Now, instead of writing a prayer that asks God to remove the problem, write a lion chasing prayer that asks God to help you see the situation from His perspective. Think in categories of life lessons you can learn, character traits you can develop, ways you can worship God through it, and opportunities that may open up for you in the future. Write your prayer here:

NOTES

embrace *{verb}*: to take up especially or gladly

uncertainty *{noun}*: the quality or state of doubt and skepticism

SECOND SAMUEL 23:20 TELLS US that Benaiah performed three mighty acts: He killed two of Moab's mightiest warriors, an Egyptian warrior, and a lion in a pit on a snowy day.

I know one thing for sure: None of these encounters were planned. Benaiah didn't wake up on the morning of his lion encounter and sketch out every detail. It wasn't scheduled in Outlook. It wasn't on his to do list. I'm not even sure it was on his wish list.

It's so easy to read about an incident that occurred 3,000 years ago and fail to appreciate the element of surprise because we know how the story ends. Most of the time we read the Bible like a textbook instead of appreciating the real-life accounts it contains. Its pages are full of romance, intrigue, danger, and uncertainty. The point is that killing the lion was not a foregone conclusion.

EMBRACING UNCERTAINTIES
SESSION FIVE

GOOD STORIES OR GOD STORIES

Hand-to-hand combat with another human is one thing. Humans have tendencies. You can predict punches and counterpunches with a high level of certainty. Savage beasts tend to be volatile and unpredictable. Their actions and reactions are less certain. Plus, you have to account for topographical, physiological, and atmospheric conditions.

How heavily was it snowing? Was it packing snow or slippery snow? What was the footing like in the pit? How about visibility? What time of day was it? How hungry was the lion? How well did Benaiah sleep the night before? Did he eat a well-balanced breakfast that morning?

There are a thousand variables, and they all add up to one thing: a high level of uncertainty. The outcome could have gone either way, heads or tails—in the most literal sense. That is what makes it such a great story— such a God-honoring story.

I'm no movie director, but it seems like the greatest movies have the highest level of uncertainty. You have to have romantic uncertainty or dramatic uncertainty if the movie is going to hold the attention of the audience. We love suspense.

I think of classic movies like *The Fugitive* or *Gladiator* where you're on the edge of your seat the entire movie. Or even *Sleepless in Seattle*—will Tom Hanks and Meg Ryan meet atop the Empire State Building after all?

It's the uncertainty that makes those movies worth watching, and I think it's uncertainty that makes life worth living. High levels of uncertainty don't just make the best movies; high levels of uncertainty make the best lives. Uncertainty is the point where faith enters the equation.

> Do you agree that high levels of uncertainty make the best lives? Why or why not?

> What uncertainties are you currently facing? Are you embracing them, ignoring them, or resisting them?

Lion-chasers need romance too. Plan a viewing of *Sleepless in Seattle* as an example of the uncertainty that makes life exciting.

Some would argue that faith results in a reduction of uncertainty. I'm only partially convinced that's true, mainly because there are different kinds of uncertainty. There are *spiritual* uncertainties and there are *circumstantial* uncertainties.

Faith does reduce spiritual uncertainty. We can know that we know that our sins are forgiven; our names are written in the Lamb's book of life; we have been adopted as God's children; every spiritual blessing is ours in Christ; and when we cross the space-time continuum, we'll spend eternity in a place called heaven.

Here's the trick: I think it's those spiritual certainties that enable us to embrace circumstantial uncertainties. Faith results in a reduction of spiritual uncertainty, but it often results in an increase in circumstantial uncertainty because God consistently calls us to go places and do things that require total reliance upon Him. In many instances, *more* faith actually results in *more* uncertainty.

Nelson's Bible Dictionary defines faith as "a belief or confident attitude toward God, involving commitment to His will for one's life." In contemporary thought, "faith" has become a word associated with self-help psychology. The difference is that this faith is rooted in a belief or confidence in oneself, while biblical faith is rooted in a belief or confidence in God.

What is the difference between spiritual uncertainty and circumstantial uncertainty?

Are you facing any spiritual uncertainties? What are they?

Are you facing any circumstantial uncertainties? What are they?

Oswald Chambers said it best: "To be certain of God is to be uncertain in all our ways. You never know what a day may bring. This is generally said with a sign of sadness; it should rather be an expression of breathless expectation."[5]

Certainty and monotony are spiritual synonyms.

I think some of us are bored to tears with our faith, and I'll tell you why—we've settled for certainty. If we actually stepped out in faith relationally or financially or spiritually, we'd be anything but bored. Go on a mission trip. Share your faith. Start tithing on your income. Quit walking the path of certainty.

"Faith is to believe what you do not see; the reward of this faith is to see what you believe."
—St. Augustine

> Hebrews 11:1 says, "Now faith is the reality of what is hoped for, the proof of what is not seen." The King James Version says it this way: "Now faith is the substance of things hoped for, the evidence of things not seen." In what areas of life do you need to have faith in God?

> Do you agree that certainty and monotony are spiritual synonyms? Why?

> Think back to the most certain and uncertain times in your life. What did your corresponding spiritual life look like?

> Are you bored or excited about your faith?

ADVENTURE

Do you remember what Jesus said to those who wanted to follow Him? He gave them a warning in Matthew 8:20:

"Foxes have dens and birds of the sky have nests, but the Son of Man has no place to lay His head."

Here is my translation: When you follow Christ, you never know where you're going to end up. Anything can happen. All bets are off. That is scary, but it is also exciting. Jesus was promising high levels of uncertainty—the element of surprise. He delivers on His promises. Following Christ is the ultimate adventure.

Read Luke 9:57—10:1. What uncertainties did each man face when considering following Christ?

Why do you think Jesus was so harsh with these men?

What did these men miss because they weren't willing to embrace the uncertainty of following Christ?

Listen to the audio file "Pushing On." Your group leader will send it to you via e-mail. Would you be willing to follow Jesus anywhere?

Which of these three men do you most identify with?

A few years ago, I took my son Parker camping for his birthday. We got to Cape Henlopen State Park around 6:30 p.m., set up camp, roasted some hot dogs, and then we went on a night hike to the Great Dune Observatory that overlooks the Delaware Bay and Atlantic Ocean.

It was a clear night so you could actually see the lights from Cape May, New Jersey, across the bay. Parker said, "Look, Dad, it's Europe." I almost didn't have the heart to tell him that it was just New Jersey!

We got up at 6:30 the next morning to watch the sunrise. Then we explored some dunes, went lizard hunting, and caught some hermit crabs on the beach.

If I had to describe our camping trip in one phrase, I'd describe it this way—never a dull moment. There is something about a camping trip that turns everything into an adventure. You aren't just eating. You're adventure eating—you cook your food over the campfire. You aren't just sleeping. You're adventure sleeping—you're in a tent under the stars. And you're not just walking. You're adventure walking—you experience mysterious sights and sounds all around you.

Can I suggest that is precisely what a relationship with Christ does? I think following Jesus ought to feel more like a camping trip. It turns everything into an adventure, and part of adventure is a high level of uncertainty.

SACRIFICING CERTAINTY

Matthew 4:18-22 records the calling of the first disciples. All of them were fishing at the time. I'm guessing they enjoyed fishing. It was the family business and all they had ever known. They were probably pretty certain of themselves when they were in the boat. When Jesus called them, Scripture says they left their boats and their father and followed Him. In a sense, Jesus was calling them to sacrifice certainty. He was telling them to leave everything they knew behind—their family, their careers, and their livelihood. I think we underestimate how tough this was.

I wonder if their families ever tried to pressure them into returning: "So when are you going to come back and take over the family business?" I wonder if they ever used the guilt card: "Dad really needs your help."

What we fail to appreciate is that following in the footsteps of your father was a cultural expectation. They were expected to carry on the family business that had probably been in the family for generations. There was a degree of security and certainty in that. Following Jesus required sacrificing their certainty.

> **Has God ever asked you to give up something? What was it, and how hard was it to release?**

The German physicist named Werner Heisenberg stated that sometimes matter behaves like a particle—it appears to be in one place at one time, and sometimes matter behaves like a wave—it appears to be in several places at the same time, almost like a wave on a pond. It is the duality of nature. The revolutionary conclusion became known as the Heisenberg Uncertainty Principle: There will always be an element of uncertainty in the universe.

Has God ever asked you to do something that disrupted your family relationships or friendships?

When we look back on our lives, the defining moments are going to be those forks in the road where we could have stayed on the path of certainty, but we made a decision to walk down the path of uncertainty instead. I suppose Peter, Andrew, James, and John could have spent the rest of their lives fishing on the Sea of Galilee, but they made a decision to walk the path of uncertainty with Jesus.

One of the toughest decisions I ever made was deciding to transfer from the University of Chicago to Central Bible College.

At the end of my freshman year, I was starting to feel the pressure to declare a major, and I realized that I had never asked God what He wanted me to do with my life. So I started praying and seeking that entire summer between my freshman and sophomore years at the University of Chicago. It was during a prayer walk through a cow pasture in Alexandria, Minnesota, that I really sensed God calling me into full-time ministry.

On paper, everything was perfect at the University of Chicago. I had a full-ride scholarship. I had a position on the basketball team. It was one of the top-rated academic institutions in the country. I knew that a degree from the U of C could open doors to lots of jobs and lots of graduate programs. It was perfect, but I really felt like God was calling me to pursue full-time ministry right away—not when I graduated.

So I transferred to Central Bible College. I had to sacrifice the certainties of the University of Chicago to pursue the uncertainties of ministry. I look back on it as one of the defining decisions of my life. I had to give up something that was good in order to experience the best that God had for me.

So here is the question: What certainties do you need to sacrifice?

Maybe it's a relationship. I had a conversation with someone not long ago, and she told me about a relationship she ended because they weren't spiritually compatible. It was so painful, but I was so proud of her. That is a hard sacrifice to make, but in the long run I believe that spiritual compatibility is at the top of the list when it comes to a healthy and holy marriage.

> List your three closest relationships. Are they moving you toward Christ or away from Christ?

Maybe you're feeling financial pressure right now. I'd encourage you to step out in faith and do something counterintuitive. Start tithing. I know it'll increase financial uncertainty, but it also gives God room to work. If you honor God with your finances, God will bless you. You can take it to the bank.

> It has been said that you can determine a person's priorities by looking at their calendar and checkbook. If someone were to examine your calendar and checkbook, what would they list as your top five priorities?

The practice of the tithe predates Mosaic Law in the Scripture. The first recorded tithe is Genesis 14:17-20 when Abraham gave the priest Melchizedek one-tenth of all the goods he had received in battle. The word "tithe" is first found in Leviticus 27:30, and it means "one-tenth."

Maybe it's occupational. I respect people who are bold enough to make a career move in their 30s or 40s or 50s. They refuse to settle for a position. They want to pursue God-ordained passions so they apply to graduate school or start over at the bottom of the totem pole.

I'm not sure what certainty you need to sacrifice, but I have one last bit of advice: *Don't wait for perfect conditions!*

"One who watches the wind will not sow, and the one who looks at the clouds will not reap" (Ecclesiastes 11:4).

In other words, if you're waiting for perfect conditions, you'll never do anything. There is a time to be cautious and a time to throw caution to the wind. There is a time to be prudent and a time to be valiant. It takes an awful lot of discernment to know when to do which.

Regardless of when you actually act, if you wait for certainty, you'll never do anything. In the words of Andy Stanley:

"There will always be an element of uncertainty. Generally speaking, you are probably never going to be more than 80 percent certain. Waiting for greater certainty may cause you to miss an opportunity.

"Uncertainty actually increases with increased leadership responsibility. The more responsibility you assume as a leader, the more uncertainty you will be expected to manage. The cost of success as a leader is greater uncertainty, not less."[6]

If Benaiah had waited for perfect conditions, he would have never chased the lion. After all, it was a snowy day.

> What certainties do you need to sacrifice? What certainties are easier to sacrifice? What certainties are more difficult to sacrifice?

THE WILD GOOSE CHASE

Kids love chasing things. It's almost like we have a chasing gene. It's part of our DNA.

As we grow up, we stop chasing butterflies and start chasing the opposite sex. Then we chase academic or athletic or artistic goals. We chase degrees. We chase dreams. Then we graduate, and we chase positions.

Finally, something happens: We stop chasing and start settling. The problem with that is stated in Proverbs 29:18a:

"Where there is no vision the people perish" (*Amplified Bible*).

In other words, when you stop chasing your God-given dream you start dying.

We need something to chase. It's the way God has wired us. Too many of us stop chasing, or we're chasing the wrong thing.

The Celtic Christians had an interesting name for the Holy Spirit. They called Him the Wild Goose. It sounds a little sacrilegious at first, but I love that name. I can't think of a better description of what it's like to be led by the Holy Spirit than a wild goose chase. When you follow the Wild Goose, you'll go places and meet people and do things you never dreamed of.

Paul acknowledged the wild goose chase in Acts 20:22:

"And now I am on my way to Jerusalem, bound in my spirit, not knowing what I will encounter there."

Look at the maps of Paul's missionary journeys in the back of your Bible, and you will see a man on a wild goose chase.

> How does the image of "wild goose chase" change your understanding of following the Holy Spirit?

On one level, God is predictable. He is the same yesterday, today, and forever. He is loving and gracious and powerful. You can take it to the bank. However, God is also predictably unpredictable. Jesus said it this way in John 3:8:

"The wind blows where it pleases, and you hear its sound, but you don't know where it comes from or where it is going. So it is with everyone born of the Spirit."

In other words, if you are Spirit-led, you will experience high levels of unpredictability.

That can cause high levels of angst or high levels of excitement. Hold that thought.

> In what ways is God predictable?

> In what ways is God unpredictable?

Have you ever experienced the Spirit leading you into high levels of unpredictability? How did that affect your faith?

I daresay that everybody reading this has something in common: You drove your parents crazy when you were a kid. Here's how you did it: You sat in the backseat of your family car, and you asked one question over and over again. You all know the question because you asked it so many times: *Are we there yet?*

I think that question reveals something about human nature. We want to know exactly where we're going, and we want to know exactly when we'll get there. That's a nice way of saying we're control freaks.

We want a complete itinerary with everything about the journey mapped out.

Unfortunately for us, as long as the Holy Spirit is in the driver's seat and we're in the backseat, we'll never know exactly where we're going or when we'll get there. I used to hate that, but I've learned to love it.

Now I think the greatest moments in life are unscripted. They are unrehearsed and unplanned and unpredictable. That's precisely what makes them unforgettable.

Let me put it in theatrical terms.

I think part of us wants God to take us to a three-act play with a clearly defined plot that has a beginning, a middle, and an end. The Holy Spirit takes us to the improv version of life instead. We want the entire script up front, but that would undermine our dependence on the Holy Spirit.

We've got to learn to enjoy the unplanned, unscripted, unpredictable moments in life. That's part and parcel of chasing the Wild Goose. It's improvisation.

Acts 1 begins with 12 dysfunctional disciples. Acts 28 ends with the gospel spreading to the entire ancient world. In between are a bunch of wild goose chases.

For Mark's own story of uncertainty, check out the short film "U-Haul" at *chasethelion.com/guide/ embracing-uncertainty*.

We want everything planned out, but God loves giving us offbeat assignments. Isn't that what Jesus did when He sent the disciples out on their first assignment in Luke 9? Listen to His instructions:

"Take nothing for the road," He told them, "no walking stick, no traveling bag, no bread, no money; and don't take an extra shirt" (Luke 9:3).

CRASH

In his book, *The Barbarian Way,* Erwin McManus writes about different animal groups. If you've studied ornithology or entomology or herpetology, you know that different groups of creatures have different names.

A group of fish is called a school. Ants are called colonies, and bees are called a swarm. Cattle are herds, birds are flocks, and a tribe of lions is a pride. For what it's worth, a group of buzzards is called a committee.

My personal favorite? A group of rhinos is called a crash.

That name seems so fitting. Believe it or not, a rhino can run about 30 miles per hour, which is pretty amazing considering how much weight they carry. They are actually faster than squirrels which can run about 26 miles per hour. Now there's a mental image.

The funny thing is that rhinos have terrible eyesight. They can only see about 30 feet in front of themselves. So they are running 30 miles an hour with no idea what's 31 feet away. You would think they'd be timid creatures because they can't see very far in front of themselves, but God, in His amazingly creative foresight, gave rhinos a big horn on the front of their heads.

Erwin McManus piggy-backs off the crash analogy: "The future is uncertain, but we need to move toward it with confidence. There's a future to be created, a humanity to be liberated. We need to stop wasting our time and stop being afraid of what we cannot see and do not know. We need to move forward full of force because of what we do know."[7]

Chase the Wild Goose.

MENTAL PREPARATION:
SCRIPTURE MEMORY

"Don't worry about anything, but in everything, through prayer and petition with thanksgiving, let your requests be made known to God" (Philippians 4:6).

SPIRITUAL PREPARATION:
PRAYER EXPERIMENT

In Acts 1:4-5, Jesus told His disciples to stay in Jerusalem and wait for the gift the Father promised. He continued, "This is what you heard from Me; for John baptized with water, but you will be baptized with the Holy Spirit not many days from now." The disciples faced a lot of uncertainty—when would this happen? Who exactly was the Holy Spirit? What would it feel like? Would they know it when it happened? Nevertheless, they remained in Jerusalem together and prayed.

Ten days later, the Holy Spirit fell on the believers at an event called Pentecost and 3,000 people were baptized into the church. You can't necessarily plan a history-making movement of the Holy Spirit like the experience of Pentecost, but you can pray.

- Over the next week, do a Pentecost Prayer Experiment. Make a list of friends and family members who are not following Christ. Pray that God would fill you with His Holy Spirit and give you the opportunity to talk to them about your faith.

NOTES

NOTES

look *{verb}*: to have an appearance that befits or accords with

foolish *{noun}*: lacking in sense, judgment or discretion

A FEW MONTHS AGO, I was reading the writings of John Muir—the founder of the Sierra Club. Though Muir is a complex individual, the love of nature was his central passion. He spent his life studying, protecting, and appreciating it.

One of my favorite Muir moments happened in December of 1874. John Muir was staying with a friend at his cabin in the Sierra Mountains, and a winter storm set in. The wind was so strong that it bent the trees over backward. Instead of retreating to the safety of the cabin, Muir chased the storm. He found a mountain ridge, climbed to the top of a giant Douglas Fir tree, and held on for dear life for several hours feasting his senses on the sights and sounds and scents.

In his journal, Muir wrote:

"When the storm began to sound I lost no time in pushing out into the woods to enjoy it. For on such occasions, Nature always has something rare to show us, and the danger to life and limb is hardly greater than one would experience crouching deprecatingly beneath a roof."[8]

John Muir was no stranger to danger. He climbed mountains and crossed rivers and explored glaciers. There is something about this mental picture of John Muir climbing a 100-foot Douglas Fir tree during a storm that is iconic.

LOOKING FOOLISH

SESSION SIX

CLIMBING TREES

In the words of Eugene Peterson, the story of John Muir climbing to the top of that storm-whipped Douglas Fir is an icon of Christian spirituality. He called it a standing rebuke against becoming a mere spectator to life, preferring creature comfort to Creator confrontation.

We are called to climb trees. It's based on more than an eccentric naturalist named John Muir. Climbing trees is actually a biblical metaphor:

"[Jesus] entered Jericho and was passing through. There was a man named Zacchaeus who was a chief tax collector, and he was rich. He was trying to see who Jesus was, but he was not able because of the crowd, since he was a short man. So running ahead, he climbed up a sycamore tree to see Jesus, since He was about to pass that way. When Jesus came to the place, He looked up and said to him, 'Zacchaeus, hurry and come down, because today I must stay at your house.'

"So he quickly came down and welcomed Him joyfully. All who saw it began to complain, 'He's gone to lodge with a sinful man!'

"But Zacchaeus stood there and said to the Lord, 'Look, I'll give half of my possessions to the poor, Lord! And if I have extorted anything from anyone, I'll pay back four times as much!'

"'Today salvation has come to this house,' Jesus told him, 'because he too is a son of Abraham. For the Son of Man has come to seek and to save the lost'" (Luke 19:1-10).

We read stories like this and don't think much of it, but how many adults do you know that still climb trees?

I love the mental picture of this tax collector in a three-piece suit climbing a tree just to get a glimpse of Jesus.

Zacchaeus had a reputation to protect. He had an image to uphold, but this distinguished tax collector climbed a tree like a little kid. He didn't care about decorum. He didn't care about protocol. He didn't care how foolish he looked. He just wanted to get a glimpse of Jesus.

I want you to notice what is often overlooked in this story: Zacchaeus was willing to look foolish to get a glimpse of Jesus. Jesus returned the favor so much so that the people criticized Him for hanging out with Zacchaeus.

"Zacchaues" means "clean" or "innocent," a hugely ironic name considering the lifestyle that the tax collector had adopted.

The end result was an amazing conversion. Zacchaeus gave half his possessions to the poor on the spot. Jesus proclaimed, "Salvation has come to your house."

This is one of those days you never forget. I'm sure Zacchaeus never forgot the day Jesus came through Jericho—the day he climbed a sycamore tree and Jesus hung out at his house. This must have become the defining moment of His life, and I think that perhaps Zacchaeus occasionally made a pilgrimage back to that tree. Maybe he even climbed it for old time's sake. I bet he brought his grandkids there and let them climb the tree and told them that was where he met Jesus.

We don't know what happened to Zacchaeus. I think that giving half his possessions to the poor was just the beginning. He could have cheated people the rest of his life and lived selfishly, but if this story is any indication, Zacchaeus decided to make a difference with his life. And it all started with climbing a tree.

Describe a time when you went to great lengths and inconvenience to catch a glimpse of Jesus.

Have you ever sacrificed your reputation in order to follow Jesus? Do you know anyone who has sacrificed their reputation in order to follow Christ?

How are giving possessions to the poor and salvation related?

During the time of this story, Jericho was a major producer and exporter of balsam. In fact, the palm groves and balsam of Jericho were so valuable that Antony gave them to Cleopatra as a source of revenue. As a tax collector in this city, Zacchaeus held an important post and would have been a very wealthy man. The Jewish people regarded him as an outcast and traitor since he was employed by and benefited from his association with the Roman occupation.

If you don't know what God is looking for, it is awfully hard to please Him. In fact, we waste a lot of effort trying to please God in ways that aren't pleasing to Him. The Pharisees are Exhibit A. God isn't looking for religious protocol; God is looking for tree climbers. He is looking for people who will do anything necessary to get to Him.

Read the Gospels, and you'll find that God is looking for tax collectors who climb trees and prostitutes who crash parties. He is looking for people who push through crowds like the woman with the issue of blood. He is looking for people who yell at the top of their lungs like the blind beggar. He is looking for people who cut holes in ceilings, jump out of boats, and follow stars to get to Jesus.

THE WILLINGNESS TO LOOK FOOLISH

Let me give you an alternate definition of faith: *Faith* is the willingness to look foolish.

It seems like the people who God uses the most are the people who are willing to climb trees or get out of boats or follow stars or chase lions. The greatest turning points in Scripture can be traced back to someone who was willing to look foolish.

Don't tell me Noah didn't feel a little foolish building an ark when rain wasn't in the forecast for another 120 years. Don't tell me David didn't feel a little foolish going to war with a slingshot. Don't tell me Benaiah didn't feel a little foolish chasing the king of beasts. Don't tell me the wise men didn't feel a little foolish when Jewish border agents asked them the reason for their visit. Don't tell me a professional fisherman didn't feel a little foolish stepping out of a boat in the middle of the lake. Don't tell me Jesus didn't feel a little foolish hanging half-naked on the cross in front of His family and friends.

Faith is the willingness to look foolish, and the results speak for themselves. Noah was saved from the flood. David defeated Goliath. The wise men found the Messiah. Peter walked on water. Jesus was raised from the dead.

What do you think about this definition of faith?

Can you think of other biblical characters who did foolish things for God?

I think the reason many of us have never killed a giant or walked on water or found the Messiah is because we're not willing to look foolish.

First Corinthians 1:27 reveals God's modus operandi:

"Instead, God has chosen the world's foolish things to shame the wise, and God has chosen the world's weak things to shame the strong."

Nothing has changed. If you aren't willing to look foolish, you're foolish.

Consider 1 Corinthians 1:27. Why do you think God operates this way?

The word "foolish" in this verse comes from the Greek word *moros*, meaning dull or stupid, heedless, absurd, and blockheaded. We get our English word "moron" form this word.

Can you think of any examples of this principle in action?

I felt a little foolish giving up a scholarship and transferring from the University of Chicago to Central Bible College. It felt a little foolish moving to Washington, D.C., with no place to live and no guaranteed salary. It felt a little foolish when we used to start services with half a dozen people. It felt like we were playing church. It felt a little foolish writing a book with no publisher. Those acts of foolishness were lions God had called me to chase.

Deep down inside, I think all of us have this primal longing to do something crazy for God. We want to build an ark or kill a giant or chase a lion. We want to do something great for God, but we allow the fear of foolishness to paralyze us.

I can't share my faith. I can't pray for a miracle. I can't get involved in a ministry. I can't seek out counseling. I can't change majors. I can't quit my job. I can't ask her out on a date. I can't raise my hand—*I might look foolish.*

It's the fear of foolishness that keeps us from walking on water or killing giants or finding the Messiah.

I wonder . . . what foolish thing is God asking you to do? In other words, what lion is God calling you to chase?

Maybe it's time to apply for your dream job; admit your addiction; reconcile the relationship; ask her out; take the exam; go on a mission trip; mentor someone; stop attending church and start serving; add a stamp to your passport; take a night class; start a business; or write the manuscript.

> Have you ever known anyone who did something for God that seemed foolish to everyone else? What did they do? How did others react?

Have you done anything for God that seemed foolish to others? How did they react to you? Did their reaction build your faith or discourage you?

What's the difference between God-directed foolishness and mere foolishness?

Is God asking you to do something foolish now? Write it down and take a moment to pray about it.

DRUNK

So how do we overcome this fear of foolishness? I think the answer is found in Ephesians 5:18:

"And don't get drunk with wine, which leads to reckless actions, but be filled with the Spirit."

What happens when people get drunk? They lose all inhibitions. Paul was saying that wine is the wrong way to lose our inhibitions. The right way is by being filled with the Holy Spirit; He will help us overcome our ungodly inhibitions. You can see a picture of it in the Book of Acts.

When the apostles were filled with the spirit, there was a boldness that compelled them to action. In fact, the same Peter who denied Jesus three times said, "We are unable to stop speaking about what we have seen and heard" (Acts 4:20). He became an unstoppable force. Why? He was filled with the Spirit of God. When we are filled with the Spirit, we care less about what people think and more about what God thinks.

The word "filled" comes from the Greek word *pleroo*, which carries with it the idea of being filled to the point of overflowing. It is the present imperative tense, which means we should keep on being filled.

Does Ephesians 5:18 change your understanding of the Holy Spirit's role in any way?

What does it mean to be filled with the Spirit? Do you think you are currently filled with the Spirit?

In general, do you care more about what other people think or about what God thinks? In what areas are you more concerned with what people think? In what areas are you more concerned with what God thinks?

Let me take you all the way back to the garden of Eden. I would suggest that there were no inhibitions in Eden before the fall of man. Adam and Eve were running around naked, and there was no shame. What happened the moment they sinned? They became self-conscious. Genesis 3:7 says:

"Then the eyes of both of them were opened, and they knew they were naked; so they sewed fig leaves together and made loincloths for themselves."

I think self-consciousness is part of the curse. The more we sin, the more self-conscious we become.

I think sanctification works the opposite way. As we are filled with the Spirit of God, we care less about what people think and more about what God thinks. We become less self-conscious and more God-conscious until we have no ungodly inhibitions.

For what it's worth, I think we'll be completely God-conscious when we get to heaven. I don't think there will be any negative self-consciousness in heaven because there will be no shame. We'll be so enraptured with the presence of God that we won't have time to waste on self-consciousness.

We have some fleeting moments of "God-consciousness" in the meantime. It is in those moments that we cease to care about appearances because we are so caught up in who God is and what He is doing in our lives. Often, a moment like that seems foolish from the outside looking in. But that doesn't really matter to the person experiencing it. If just for a moment, that person is real. They are raw. They are fully authentic.

> **What is the difference between being God-conscious and self-conscious? Which are you more prone to be?**

> **Have you ever experienced a moment of "God-consciousness"? Was it simply a fleeting mountain-top experience, or did it have a lasting impact? How?**

"Sanctification" is a theological word that describes the spiritual growth process that happens after we cross the line of faith. It's the process by which we become more like Christ. In *Christian Beliefs*, Wayne Grudem defines sanctification as a progressive work of both God and man that makes Christians more and more free from sin and more and more like Christ in their actual lives.

CAGED CHRISTIANS

A few months ago, I was in the Galapagos Islands on a mission trip. Though it's hard to describe, it felt like we were flying into the garden of Eden. I think that this archipelago of islands is the closest thing to Eden left on earth. It doesn't feel like the islands belong to the people. It feels like they belong to the animals; the animals just allow the people to live there. It was almost like going to the zoo except there were no cages or fences.

Listen to "Fool for You" by Nicole Nordeman. When was the last time you looked like a fool for the sake of Christ?

There is nothing like seeing a wild animal in its natural habitat. It's one thing to see a caged bird. It's an altogether different thing to see a blue-footed booby circling in the air and dive-bomb into the ocean to catch a fish mere feet from your boat.

It's one thing seeing a dolphin show in a man-made pool. It is an altogether different thing swimming with sea lions or walking a beach at night with dozens of them barking and chasing you. We were surrounded by huge tortoises, beautiful marine iguanas, and pelicans that looked pre-historic. Part of the excitement was the fact that they weren't caged.

After returning from the Galapagos, we took our kids to the zoo, and you know what? It wasn't the same. I love zoos, but I'm ruined for them now. It's not the same seeing a caged animal. It's too safe. It's too controlled. It's too predictable.

As we were walking through the ape house, I had this thought as I looked at a caged gorilla: *I wonder if churches do to people what zoos do to animals?*

We take something that is wild, and we domesticate it. We put it in a cage for easy observation. We remove the danger. We remove the risk. The end result is caged Christians.

What do you think about the image of caged Christians?

Do you ever feel like a caged Christian?

It just seems to me that isn't the approach Jesus took. For starters, He handpicked a dozen disciples who were totally uncultured, uncivilized, and undomesticated. Jesus didn't cage people—He unleashed them.

In fact, He used a zoological metaphor in Matthew 10:16a. As He was about to send them on their inaugural mission, He said, "Look, I'm sending you out like sheep among wolves." Imagine a zookeeper putting a bunch of sheep in the wolf cage. Now there's a zoo worth visiting.

Jesus didn't put the disciples in a safe cage; He unleashed them. He sent them into the wolf cage saying they should be as harmless as doves and shrewd as serpents.

The goal of church shouldn't be to take people out of their natural habitat and domesticate them—make them look and talk and act like Christians. When we pronounce the benediction at the end of the service, we're releasing people back into the wild. You go back into your natural habitat as an ambassador of God's grace.

I love the way Erwin McManus says it in his book, *Unstoppable Force:* "The center of God's will is not a safe place but the most dangerous place in the world." Then he makes a great distinction: "To live outside of God's will puts us in danger; to live in His will makes us dangerous."[9]

> **Do you agree or disagree with Erwin's statement that to "live outside of God's will puts us in danger; to live in His will makes us dangerous"?**

> **Why does living outside God's will put us in danger?**

Which of the following foolish things do you need to do? Check three and list the due date for each.

- ❏ Tell someone you're sorry.
- ❏ Fast.
- ❏ Confess a sin.
- ❏ Share your faith with a friend.
- ❏ Tithe.
- ❏ Serve in the church or community.
- ❏ Go on a mission trip.
- ❏ Tell someone you love them.
- ❏ Lead a small group.
- ❏ Befriend a homeless person.
- ❏ Ask for a raise or a new responsibility at work.
- ❏ Ask someone out.
- ❏ Sell something and give the money to someone in need.
- ❏ Pray every day.
- ❏ Pursue a new hobby.
- ❏ Submit your resignation.
- ❏ Submit your résumé for a new job.
- ❏ Go back to school.
- ❏ Other_____
- ❏ Other_____
- ❏ Other_____

You can choose to be unleashed. You can break out of the cage of safety. It might be a little dangerous and a little risky, but outside of those bars is where you will find the kind of abundant life that Jesus promises.

In a culture obsessed with self-protection and safety, you can choose to run after opportunities instead of letting them come to you. You can embrace uncertainty instead of seeking to eliminate it. You can choose to take risks rather than minimize them. You can confront your fears instead of hiding from them. You can reframe adversity instead of letting it dominate you. And you can embrace foolishness as a mark of following Christ. In short, you have the choice to chase the lions that confront you rather than running away.

So go ahead—start chasing and start living.

MENTAL PREPARATION:
SCRIPTURE MEMORY

"Instead, God has chosen the world's foolish things to shame the wise" (1 Corinthians 1:27a).

SPIRITUAL PREPARATION:
PRAYER EXPERIMENT

○ The following prayer would probably be considered foolish because 1) it asks God to expose sin, and 2) asks God to lead us (and we've seen from Scripture where that has taken people!). This is a dangerous, lion-chasing prayer. Pray it every day over the next week:

"Search me, God, and know my heart; test me and know my concerns. See if there is any offensive way in me; lead me in the everlasting way" (Psalm 139:23-24).

NOTES

NOTES

END NOTES

SESSION 1

1 http://ted.aol.com

2 Gilovich and Mevec, "The Temporal Pattern"; T. Gilovich and V.H. Medvec, "The Experience of Regret: What, When, and Why," Psychological Review 102 (1995): 379-95.

SESSION 2

3 Howard Schultz, *Pour Your Heart Into It* (New York: Hyperion, 1999), 63.

SESSION 4

4 *The Third Man* (232).

SESSION 5

5 Oswald Chambers, *My Utmost for His Highest* (Westwood: Barbour and Company, 2006), 120.

6 Andy Stanley, *The Next Generation Leader* (Sisters: Multnomah Publishers, 2006), 78-79.

7 Erwin Raphael McManus, *The Barbarian Way* (Nashville: Nelson Books, 2005) 68-69,138.

SESSION 6

8 http://library.untraveledroad.com/Bk/Muir/Mountains.html

9 Erwin Raphael McManus, *Unstoppable Force* (Orange: Yates & Yates, 2001) 31-33.

What is Threads?

WE ARE A COMMUNITY OF YOUNG ADULTS— people who are piecing the Christian life together, one experience at a time. We're rooted in Romans 12 and Colossians 3. We're serious about worshipping God with our lives. We want to understand the grace Jesus extended to us on the cross and act on it. We want community, need to worship, and aren't willing to sit on our hands when the world needs help. We want to grow. We crave Bible study that raises questions, makes us think, and causes us to own our faith. We're interested in friendships that are as strong as family ties—the kind of relationships that transform individuals into communities.

Our Bible studies are built for young adults, featuring flexible formats with engaging supplemental video and audio, four- to six-week sessions to fit into busy schedules, and supplemental resources for members and leaders online. These discussion-driven studies intentionally foster group and individual connections and encourage practical application of Scripture.

We don't expect you to come up with the tools you need to lead these engaging discussions in your communities on your own. We've designed a separate **Leader Kit**— or expansion pack as we like to call it—that contains all the stuff you normally have to go out looking for when you want to explore a topic. Purchase the Kit and you'll receive theme-related videos, audio clips, and music in formats that are flexible for your group, along with a **Leader Guide** in PDF format and other articles and tools that encourage practical application of Scripture. You'll also find topical articles, staff and author blogs, podcasts, and lots of other great resources at:

threadsmedia.com

Stop by to join our online community — and come by to visit often!

THE TOUGH SAYINGS OF JESUS
by Michael Kelley

This study explores four things Jesus said that are difficult to comprehend. Delving into the historical and cultural contexts of these Scriptures, the study focuses on sparking discussion and providing fresh insight, instead of pat answers. It will encourage you to embrace your doubts, and process through them, so that your faith can become deeper and stronger.

Michael Kelley is a writer and traveling communicator who speaks to students and young adults throughout the United States. Passionate about effectively communicating the fullness of the good news of Jesus, Michael previously served as the principle teacher for Refuge, a weekly worship event for young adults in Nashville, Tennessee. Visit him at www.michaelkelleyonline.com.

GET UNCOMFORTABLE:
SERVE THE POOR. STOP INJUSTICE.
CHANGE THE WORLD ... IN JESUS' NAME.
by Todd Phillips

Phillips guides you to understand how your faith in Christ and concern for the poor go hand-in-hand. As he examines God's character and perspective regarding poverty and injustice, he offers an understanding of what God calls you to do, along with practical ways to impact culture by caring for "the least of these."

Todd Phillips is the teaching pastor of Frontline, the young adult ministry of McLean Bible Church near Washington D.C. His passions are teaching the people of God and sharing the Gospel with those who aren't yet Christians. He is the author of Spiritual CPR: Reviving a Flat-lined Generation.

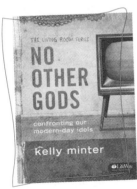

NO OTHER GODS:
CONFRONTING MODERN DAY IDOLS
by Kelly Minter

Do you worship the one true God, while also serving a bunch of smaller gods? No Other Gods: Confronting Our Modern-Day Idols is a Bible study for people seeking a place to openly talk about the little gods that take up our time, occupy space in our hearts, and impact our ability to serve. This study is designed to take place in a comfortable living room filled with friends, conversation, and good food—simple, yummy recipes and leader guide included in book.

Kelly Minter is committed to using her talents and gifts to move people further along in their relationship with God. As a songwriter, worship leader, speaker, and author, Kelly travels extensively across the country. Find out more about the ministry of Kelly Minter at www.kellyminter.com.

**For full details on all of Threads'
studies, visit www.threadsmedia.com.**

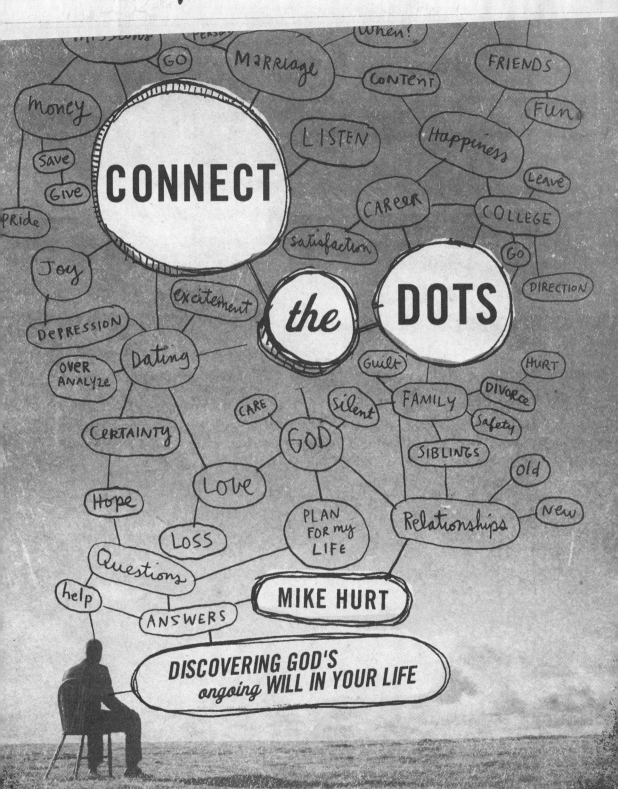

CONNECT the DOTS

MIKE HURT

DISCOVERING GOD'S ongoing WILL IN YOUR LIFE

TABLE of CONTENTS

Introduction
"Beyond the Big Three" 8
Does God really want to answer my big questions?

Session 1
"The Nature of God's Will" 12
What am I looking for anyway?

Session 2
"God's Will for Every Day" 26
How can I hear God's voice?

Session 3
"God's Will in All Seasons" 40
What about fleeces, doors, and signs?

Session 4
"God's Will Through His Spirit" 58
How does the Holy Spirit help me find God's will?

Session 5
"God's Will Through Community" 74
Is it OK to listen to other people?

Session 6
"The Silence of God" 92
What about when there's nothing to hear?

Meet the Author

MIKE HURT

My name is Mike, and I live in Leesburg, Virginia, with my wife, Kristi, and our three kids. I am on staff at McLean Bible Church (*www. mcleanbible.org*), just outside of Washington, D.C. In my role as director of community campus development, I am leading our church to become one church with multiple locations. Day in and day out, I have the unique opportunity to lead our church to multiply and thrive throughout the D.C. area. Before taking on my current role, I was the small groups pastor for McLean Bible Church and Frontline, our young adult ministry. Raised in Louisana, I graduated with a Master of Divinity from Southwestern Baptist Theological Seminary. Previously, I served as an associate pastor at Parkway Church, an innovative church plant in Victoria, Texas.

I am convinced that to work hard you must play hard or maybe just watch a lot of TV. When I'm not working or catching up on all that TiVo® has to offer, I love to be outside, build relationships with my neighbors, and play with my kids. I am a confessed technology and email addict.

It has been a very humbling process to write this book. To think that God would use me to help you know and live His will for your life amazes me. As you read and discuss *Connect the Dots*, I hope you find not just what you are looking for but what God has in store for you.

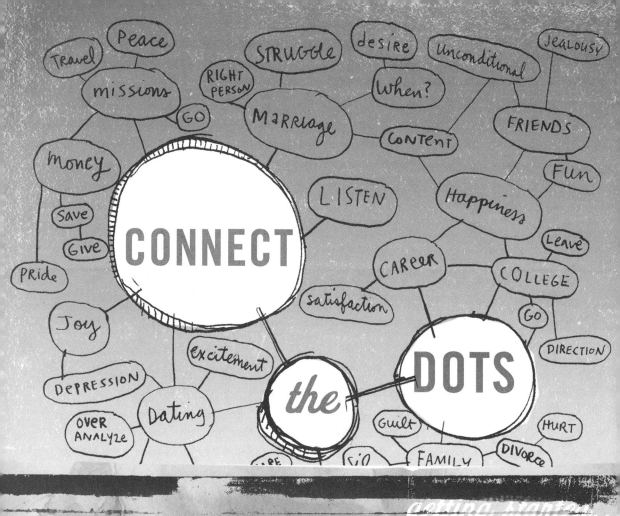

BEYOND THE BIG THREE

NOTHING SEEMS TO MOTIVATE A SEARCH FOR HIGHER PURPOSE THAN THE "BIG THREE." AS A PASTOR, I HAVE BEEN MEETING WITH YOUNG ADULTS FOR 15 YEARS. DURING THAT TIME, I HAVE LEARNED THAT THE BIG THREE . . .

WHO SHOULD I MARRY? WHERE SHOULD I WORK? AND WHERE SHOULD I LIVE?—CONSISTENTLY MOVE PEOPLE TO START ASKING THE SEEMINGLY SIMPLE QUESTION: "WHAT IS GOD'S WILL FOR MY LIFE?"

If you are asking these questions, you are certainly not alone—especially if you have spent a couple of years in the workplace and are wondering where you go from here. These are natural questions to ask; it's a part of growing in wisdom. It's a part of defining how you are going to live your life. It's a part of learning what it means to be you on your terms.

But perhaps that is also the flaw in the big three questions. It seems to me that we want to know God's will as long as His will lines up nicely with our idea of what our life should generally be like. That's usually why the big three prompt us to ask the question of God's will—we have in our minds and hearts what we want the answer to be. If that is true, then our question is not really, "What is God's will for my life?" Instead, it's "Does God's will for my life line up with my vision for my life?"

The result is a jumbled blend of our ideas and God's ideas, our desires and His desires, our will and His will. Further complicating the situation is the reality that very few of us have ever seen the proverbial skywriting telling us exactly where to work or who to marry. Many more of us have asked for God to answer our big life questions, but at the end of the day, we have simply had to make a decision with little more than a sense of which direction God wants us to go. The search for any amount of certainty or confidence in God's will has become little more than a pipe dream for most of us. Like a carrot just out of reach of the horse's nose, we ask these big questions hoping to hear a cosmic voice affirm some direction, and yet that voice always seems to be just out of earshot.

Despite this, I firmly believe that God cares deeply about the big decisions of your life. Furthermore, I believe He is incredibly concerned about the mundane, ordinary moments of your life—so much so that perhaps the question God wants us to ask is slightly different than the one we are asking right now.

MAYBE, BECAUSE GOD WANTS TO BE INTIMATELY INVOLVED IN EVERY DETAIL OF YOUR LIFE, THE QUESTION WE SHOULD BE ASKING IS NOT, "WHAT IS GOD'S WILL *FOR* MY LIFE?" BUT "WHAT IS GOD'S WILL *IN* MY LIFE?"

The difference is huge. If you are asking for God's will for your life, then you are looking for a crystal ball. You want to see into the future to try and find the most prosperous way to go. But if you recognize that God's will is not only *for* your life but *in* your life, then you are choosing to believe in a God who is more than just a fortune-teller. You are choosing to believe that God's greatest call is not for you to be married or single, a preacher or a doctor, to live in Miami or Beijing. His greatest call is for you to follow Jesus—every moment.

Maybe the next several weeks can be a time for you to rediscover that God doesn't just have a plan for you but that God cares deeply about you. Sometimes in the discussion of God's will, we can lose sight of God's love and kindness. If all we are looking for is God's will for our lives, then we betray our perception of God. Our questions reveal that we believe that God is very interested in what we do, where we go, and what we can accomplish on His behalf in the world. But is He only interested in us to the extent that we can be useful to Him?

But I believe God is much more interested in who we are than what we do. For this reason, we do not seek to find answers as much as we seek to find God Himself. It is only through our journey together with Him that we find answers, but amazingly, those answers will become of secondary importance to the great joy and satisfaction of just walking in relationship with God.

That's why it's so vital that we are convinced of God's love for us. Much in the same way that we do not just want answers from Him, He does not just want performance from us. We are meant for each other—us and God—and not just so that we can accomplish each other's desires. We are meant to walk with each other. We are meant to be in each other's lives. We are meant to live deeply together.

I hope that, for you, the end result of *Connect the Dots* is a greater love for, hope in, and commitment to the will of God in your life.

GROUP CONTACT
INFORMATION

Name _____ Number _____
Email _____

Name _____ Number _____
Email _____

Name _____ Number _____
Email _____

Name _____ Number _____
Email _____

Name _____ Number _____
Email _____

Name _____ Number _____
Email _____

Name _____ Number _____
Email _____

Name _____ Number _____
Email _____

Name _____ Number _____
Email _____

Name _____ Number _____
Email _____

GROUP CONTACT
INFORMATION

Name _____ Number _____

Email _____

Name _____ Number _____

Email _____

Name _____ Number _____

Email _____

Name _____ Number _____

Email _____

Name _____ Number _____

Email _____

Name _____ Number _____

Email _____

Name _____ Number _____

Email _____

Name _____ Number _____

Email _____

Name _____ Number _____

Email _____

Name _____ Number _____

Email _____